Franklin Benjamin Hough

Historical Sketch of Union College

Founded at Schnectady, N. Y., February 25, 1795

Franklin Benjamin Hough

Historical Sketch of Union College
Founded at Schnectady, N. Y., February 25, 1795

ISBN/EAN: 9783337060817

Printed in Europe, USA, Canada, Australia, Japan

Cover: Foto ©ninafisch / pixelio.de

More available books at **www.hansebooks.com**

Historical Sketch

OF

UNION COLLEGE.

[NOW A BRANCH OF UNION UNIVERSITY.]

FOUNDED AT SCHENECTADY, N. Y., FEBRUARY 25, 1795.

Prepared in compliance with an invitation from the Commissioner of the Bureau of Education, representing the Department of the Interior in matters relating to the National Centennial of 1876.

WASHINGTON:
GOVERNMENT PRINTING OFFICE.
1876.

PREFATORY.

DEPARTMENT OF THE INTERIOR,
BUREAU OF EDUCATION,
Washington, D. C., January 27, 1876.

This summary of the history of Union College is sent out as a specimen of the work being done in preparation for the Centennial of 1876, and as covering the leading points of inquiry embraced in a series of circulars issued from the Bureau of Education, inviting the co-operation of colleges and universities in the attempt to collect a full series of statistical and historical materials for this occasion. The returns will be aggregated in general tables, and, under the direction of Dr. Franklin B. Hough, of this Bureau, such generalizations and illustrations will be prepared with a view to publication in a final report, as the materials may warrant.

JOHN EATON,
Commissioner.

UNION COLLEGE.

ORGANIZATION AND EARLY HISTORY.

The only college within the colony of New York before
the Revolution was King's College, of New York City, which
was re-organized soon after the peace as Columbia College.
The rapid growth of settlements toward the north and west
had suggested to thoughtful minds the pressing need of some
institution for superior instruction at a convenient point in
the interior, and this idea of central accommodation for all
interests, not many years later, led to the removal of the State
capital to Albany.

Even in the midst of the Revolution we find the project of
a college at Schenectady seriously entertained,* but it did
not gain sufficient strength to secure actual existence until

---

* From a manuscript in the New York State Library, (Clinton Papers,
No. 3467,) it appears that. in compliance with petitions circulated in 1779,
a project was started for the incorporation of Clinton College at Schenectady. The preamble of the charter as then proposed is as follows:

"Whereas a great number of respectable inhabitants of the counties
of Albany, Tryon, (Montgomery,) and Charlotte, (Washington,) taking
into consideration the great benefit of a good education, the disadvan-
tages they labor under for want of the means of acquiring it, and the loud
call there now is, and no doubt will be in a future day, for men of learning to fill the several offices of church and state, and looking upon the
town of Schenectady in every respect the most suitable and commodious
seat for a seminary of learning in this State, or perhaps in America, have
presented their humble petition to the governor and legislature of this
State, earnestly requesting that a number of gentlemen may be incorporated in a body politic who shall be empowered to erect an academy or

some years after the peace. A project like this is seldom discussed without exciting local interests, and before the choice fell upon the quiet old Dutch town on the Mohawk, the claims of Poughkeepsie, Albany, and Waterford were strongly urged as suitable points for the establishment of a college in the interior, but not to the extent of dividing the effort which was for the common benefit of all.

A beginning in literary life at Schenectady was made in the formation of an association for mental improvement and debate in 1793, and on the 29th of January, 1793, a classical and scientific school was incorporated by the regents of the university under the name of "The Trustees of the

---

college in the place aforesaid, to hold sufficient funds for its support, to make proper laws for its government, and to confer degrees."

The feature of this charter (which never passed the seals) most worthy of notice is, that it contemplated the creation of a corporate body by an executive act, therein following the colonial precedents. Seven years later the regents of the university were created in nearly their present form, and empowered to grant charters to colleges and academies. The proposed corporators of Clinton College were: Eliphalet Ball, Barent Vrooman, Thomas Romaine, John Rodgers, Eilardus Westerlo, Daniel Gross, John Livingston, Alexander Miller, Philip Schuyler, James Duane, Robert R. Livingston, Abraham Ten Broeck, Abraham Yates, jr., Robert Yates, Levi Pauling, Dirck Brinckerhoff, Isaac Vrooman, Christopher Yates, John Cuyler, Henry Glen, Jacobus Teller, Hugh Mitchell, Andrew McFarlan, Abraham Oothoudt, Dirck Van Ingen, James Gordon, Robert Van Rensselaer, Pieter Vrooman, Peter Waggoner, jr., and Ebenezer Clark, of the State of New York; —— Ashley, of New Hampshire, and Timothy Edwards, of Massachusetts. The annual income of funds was to be limited to £3,000 sterling, and the president must be of the Protestant Reformed faith. The journals of the legislature show that the petitions upon which this project was founded were signed by 850 inhabitants of Tryon and Albany counties, and by 140 of Charlotte County. It is reasonable to suppose that this early attempt was not entirely abortive, since it must have created a general impression that a college would some day be established in the interior, and that Schenecady would be a proper site.

Academy in the Town of Schenectady."* A building was erected on the northwest corner of what are now Union and Ferry streets,† and in 1793 a school was opened under the care of Col. John Taylor, of New Jersey. This academy appears to have been conducted with much ability, and being well sustained by the community in which it was planted, became the germ of the college, which, fifteen years before, had been an object of earnest effort and active discussion; nor can we doubt that through these years of hope deferred the favorite thought was cherished, until the plan was fully realized.

The legislature having vested in the regents of the university the right of granting college charters, a memorial was addressed to that board by the trustees of the academy, which led to the granting of a charter to twenty-four persons therein named, and their successors, under the title of "The Trustees of Union College in the Town of Schenectady, in the State of New York."‡ They were empowered to hold

---

* In this early effort the Rev. Dirck Romeyn, pastor of the Reformed Dutch church at Schenectady, deserves honorable mention. He had much at heart the founding of a college under the patronage of his own denomination, as proposed in the movement of 1779–'80. He was pastor at this place twenty years, and died April 16, 1804.

† This building was of brick, two stories in height, about 50 by 30 feet on the ground, and cost about $3,000. It was used as the first and only building for Union College until 1804.

‡ The first trustees were Robert Yates, Abraham Yates, jr., Abraham Ten Broeck, Goldsbrow Banyar, John V. Henry, George Merchant, Stephen Van Rensselaer, John Glen, Isaac Vrooman, Joseph C. Yates, James Shuter, Nicholas Veeder, James Gordon, Beriah Palmer, Samuel Smith, Henry Walton, Ammi Rodgers, Aaron Condict, Jacobus V. C. Romeyn, James Cochran, John Frey, D. Christopher Pick, Jonas Platt, and Jonas Coe. Of these seven resided in Albany, six in Schenectady, three in Ballston, and in Saratoga, Troy, Kinderhook, Palatine, Herkimer, and Whitestown, N. Y., and Hackensack, N. J., one each. Originally there were no State officers holding *ex officio* as trustees;

an estate with an income of $13,333⅓, were vested with the
usual powers of a college, and were empowered to fill vacancies in their board by election of the remaining members.
The trustees of the academy were, a few days after, allowed
to vest their property in the college.*

The name " Union College " was given as expressing the
intention of uniting all religious sects in a common interest
for the common good by offering equal advantages to all,
with preference to none. It was designed to found an
institution upon the broad basis of Christian unity, and this
idea has ever since been faithfully followed in the spirit of
the original intention, no particular religious denomination
having at any time claimed or attempted to control its
management, or to influence the choice of trustees or
faculty. It is believed that this was the first college in
the United States not confessedly denominational in its
character.

---

but under an act passed March 30, 1805, the charter was amended by the
regents, March 29, 1806, by reducing the number to twenty-one, and
adding the chancellor, justices of the supreme court, secretary of state,
comptroller, treasurer, attorney-general, and surveyor-general, by virtue
of their civil offices. The constitution of 1821, by reducing the number
of the judges, made further vacancies, which, by an act passed February 14,
1823, were to be filled by the governor and lieutenant-governor. The
constitution of 1846, by abolishing some of the above offices, required
further changes, and the *ex-officio* trustees are now the governor, lieutenant-
governor, attorney-general, secretary of state, comptroller, and treasurer.

*Act of April 6, 1795, allowing the trustees of the academy to con-
vey, and those of the college to accept, upon which the corporate powers
of the former ceased. From the regents' records it appears that the
academy received two apportionments from the literature fund, one of
$310, in 1793, and the other of $400, in 1794.

The chronicles of the day record that the event of receiving a college
charter was celebrated by great rejoicing, with the ringing of bells, display of flags, bonfires, and a general illumination.

The college was organized on the 19th of October, by the election of the Rev. John Blair Smith, D.D., of Philadelphia, as president;* John Taylor, A.M., as professor of mathematics and natural philosophy; and the Rev. Andrew Yates, as professor of Latin and Greek languages.

The first commencement was held in May, 1797, and the first degree conferred upon three young men who had finished the course of study then required. This was an occasion of signal and novel interest to all the country around, and drew together a large and enthusiastic audience.†

Dr. Smith was succeeded by the Rev. Jonathan Edwards, D.D.,‡ who died in 1801, and was followed by the Rev. Jonathan Maxcy, D.D.,§ who resigned in 1804.

Although frequent changes are generally adverse to pros-

---

* Dr. Smith was a son of Rev. Robert Smith, a Presbyterian clergyman of Pequa, Pa., and was born June 12, 1756. He was graduated at Princeton, in 1773; studied theology with his brother, the Rev. Samuel Stanhope Smith, president of the Hampden Sidney College in Virginia, where, in 1779, he succeeded as principal. In December, 1791, he was installed over the Third Presbyterian Church in Philadelphia, to which charge he returned after leaving Union College, and died there August 22, 1799, aged 43 years.

† The first commencement exercises were held in the old Reformed Dutch Church, which continued to be the only place for these occasions during many years. Afterward the Presbyterian Church was used on alternate years, and this custom still prevails. The old Dutch Church was replaced in 1814 by a building burned in 1861, and this has since been rebuilt, in beautiful architectural style, rendering it peculiarly well adapted to commencement exercises.

‡ Mr. Edwards was born at Northampton, Mass., May 26, 1745, O.S., and was the second son of the Rev. Jonathan Edwards, afterward president of the College of New Jersey. He was graduated in 1765, and, after serving as tutor and professor, he took charge of a church at New Haven, Conn., in 1769, and at Colebrook, Conn., in 1796. He died at Schenectady, August 1, 1801.

§ Mr. Maxcy was born in Attleborough, Mass., September 2, 1768; was graduated at Brown University in 1787, appointed professor of

perity, and although the college was still feeble, it was not without enterprise. Under the presidency of Dr. Edwards, a new edifice was begun, on a scale magnificent for that day and still one of the finest and best-built in the city. An event, however, occurred in 1804 which proved to be of peculiar advantage to the institution, and from which its success may be justly dated. This event was the choice of the Rev. Eliphalet Nott,* as president. Mr. Nott was then a

divinity in 1791, and in 1792 became pastor of the First Baptist Church in Providence. Upon leaving Union College he went to South Carolina, as president of the South Carolina College at Columbia, S. C., and remained till his death, June 4, 1820, aged 52 years. A monument is erected to his memory on the college campus of the University of South Carolina, at Columbia, S. C.

* Dr. Nott was born at Ashford, Conn., June 25, 1773; received his first degree in the arts at Brown University in 1793, having gained his education under circumstances of peculiar difficulty; studied theology with the Rev. Joel Benedict, of Plainfield, Conn., and, in 1796, became pastor of a church, and teacher of a classical school at Cherry Valley, N. Y. His talents soon gained him a call to the Presbyterian church in Albany, where he remained until 1804. His wider opportunities there found a congenial field for the display of the extraordinary powers of pulpit eloquence, which he possessed, and while in this office he made perhaps the most fortunate effort of his life, in a sermon on the death of Hamilton at the hand of Burr. From this time he was looked upon as one of the rising powers of the age, and he was soon after chosen president of Union College, with which institution his name was ever after closely identified. He held this office with distinguished success the unbroken term of sixty-two years. During this long course of years, nearly four thousand students received their diplomas, and entered upon the active duties of life, becoming, in their turn, as talent and opportunity favored, centers of influence and very many of them distinguished ornaments to society in every field of honorable ambition and noble achievement. The powers of a life devoted to active mental labors gradually yielded to the infirmities of age, until terminated by death on the 29th day of January, 1866.

Had Dr. Nott given his time and energies to scientific discovery and business management, he would have doubtless won both wealth and honors in ample degree. His inventive genius applied to the construc-

young clergyman of Albany, known at the time as an eloquent and effective public speaker of dignified and courteous manners and distinguished learning, but not as yet known for that talent in the education of young men which this election gave him the opportunity to exercise and which has scarcely been surpassed in the history of any American college. Endowed by nature with a keen perception of character, a discriminating judgment. in developing latent talent, a dignity of manners commanding both love and respect, a facility in 'governing young men, wherein the secret lay in teaching them to govern themselves, and a zeal and earnestness in the discharge of every duty, he acquired and held, through a long and active life, a commanding position as an educator which was felt and acknowledged throughout the country.

Dr. Nott found the college wanting both means and students. The inhabitants of Schenectady had proposed an endowment of $30,000 in lands, obligations, and money; but the largest subscription was only $250, the next $100, and the total sum altogether, from sources other than direct gift of the State, but $42,043.74. Some grants were made by the State in years as below specified.* The building begun

---

tion of stoves for burning mineral coal led to the first great success in this line of useful discovery, and his plans for the improvement of steam navigation proved the soundness of his philosophical reasoning and his distinguished ability as an inventor.

*Act of April 9, 1795, for books and apparatus.	$3, 750 00
Act of April 11, 1796, for buildings	10, 000 00
Act of March 30, 1797, for salaries during two years	1, 500 00
Act of March 7, 1800, for completion of building	10, 000 00
Act of March 7, 1800, ten lots of 550 acres each, in the military tract, for support of president and professors	43, 483 93
Act of April 8, 1801, and April 3, 1802, sale of garrison lands near Lake George.	9, 378 20
Total State grants before 1804	78, 112 13

under Dr. Edwards's presidency was still unfinished, and the
college was burdened with a heavy debt.*

The means that had been provided were, of course,
quite inadequate to the wants of a prosperous college, and
to supply the needed endowment recourse was had to an
expedient now forbidden by a better public sentiment, but
then deemed proper for raising funds in aid of every religious, educational, and benevolent enterprise of the day, and
for every public improvement.

King's College, in New York City, had already been
aided to funds by a public lottery, but other institutions had
since arisen which had received no such aid. It was therefore deemed advisable to urge the passage of a law, which

---

* The building referred to in the text, and known in after years as "West
College," was begun in 1798 and finished in 1804. It is in the Italian style
of architecture, and probably from the designs of Philip Hooker, then an
eminent architect of Albany. It is of stone, three stories high, besides a high
basement, and is surmounted by an elegant central cupola. The ground
plan measures 150 by 60 feet, and the original cost was about $56,000,
besides $4,000 for the site. It contained a residence for the president,
the chapel, library, and recitation-rooms, and a considerable number of
dormitories. In 1815 it was sold to the city and county for a court-house,
jail, and city offices, and while thus owned it was commonly known as
the "City Hall." The college received in payment 3,000 acres of land in
detached parcels in various parts of Schenectady County. In 1831 it was
repurchased by the college for $10,000, and used for the library, cabinets,
and residence of freshman and sophomore classes until 1854. It was
then resold to the city for the sum of $6,000, and is now in use by the
city union schools. Between 1805 and 1810 a row of two-story brick
buildings was erected on College street for use as dormitories. It was
known as "Long College," and was sold about 1830. A one-story brick
building, about 30 by 80 feet, was erected by the city in the rear of the
old college (while used as a court-house) for a Lancasterian school. It
was afterward fitted up for the college cabinets and is still in use by the
city schools.

was secured March 30, 1805, for raising the sum of $80,000 by lottery.*

A few years' experience showed that the location in the city was not sufficiently ample, and the observing eye of Dr. Nott, at an early period in his presidency, had noticed in the suburbs a better one that combined in rare degree every advantage desirable. On the eastern border of the city the fields rise by a gentle slope to a plain of moderate elevation and of easy access. Near the upper edge of this slope the construction of a terrace a few feet high would afford a level campus of ample space, and a site for buildings that would overlook the valley, the river, and the neighboring city, while northward glimpses of mountains blue from distance, and southwestward ranges of hills dividing the waters of the Mohawk and Susquehanna Rivers, would present a panorama of peculiar loveliness. A gently murmuring brook issuing from dense woodlands flowed across the grounds just north of the proposed site, and in the rear alternating fields and groves extended several miles eastward to the Hudson.

A tract of some two hundred and fifty acres was secured and new buildings begun upon plans drawn by M. Ramée, a French engineer then eminent in the country, and for a time employed by the National Government in planning fortifications and public works. Construction was begun on

---

* This sum was to be drawn at four successive lotteries of $20,000 each. The act directed $35,000 to be applied to the erection of additional buildings; an equal sum to be invested upon bond and mortgage, the interest to be applied to the support of professorships; and the remaining $10,000 to be invested, one-half of the proceeds for a classical library, and the balance toward defraying the expenses of indigent scholars. Some changes in the law were afterward made, relating to the mode of investment, and for anticipating the payment of moneys that were becoming due. It appears from a legislative report made in 1814, (Assembly Journal, 1814, p. 118,) that but $55,000 were realized from this grant.

College Hill in 1812, and the buildings were so far advanced that they could be occupied in the summer of 1814. To provide the means for these improvements and for a substantial endowment, application was made for another grant of a kind similar to the last. An act was accordingly passed, largely through the efforts of Dr. Nott, for raising the sum of $200,000 for Union College, and considerable sums for other institutions.* The proceedings consequent upon these transactions extended through many years, and the drawings of the lotteries were not entirely closed until the end of 1833.

From the time of the completion of buildings on the new site, and the re-occupation of West College, no event of special interest occurred to mark the history of the institution for many years. The accompanying tables represent a season of general prosperity, and the unusually large proportion in

---

* Of the sum allowed to Union College by the act of 1814, there was specially given :

For the erection of buildings............................... $100,000
For paying an existing debt............................... 30,000
For library and apparatus 20,000
For the relief of indigent students........................ 50,000
 Total, including all sums previously given by the State, $331,612.13.

There was also assigned in the lottery grant of 1814, the sum of $40,000 to Hamilton College, $4,000 to the Asbury African church of New York, and $33,000 to the College of Physicians and Surgeons of the City of New York.

An act passed April 5, 1822, allowed the institutions in interest to assume conjointly or to appoint one of their number to complete these transactions and assume the responsibilities, the State being absolved from all liabilities that might occur therein. Union College undertook to close up the business, at which time the sum allowed to be raised was $322,256.81, of which $45,279.74 belonged to Hamilton College, and $17,000 were afterward paid, amounting to $62,279.74; the sum of $33,971.56 belonged to the College of Physicians and Surgeons, $4,529.30 to the Asbury church, and $12,000 to the New York Historical Society, making in all $112,780.62 to be deducted from the total sum that then remained to be raised.

the senior classes shows a fact well known throughout the country, that many students, after passing through the lower classes elsewhere, came hither to enjoy the instruction of Dr. Nott, and receive from him their first degree.*

Although prominence is given to the personal influence of its president, during many years of prosperity, justice requires us to record the fact, which all the graduates will indorse, that a large measure of gratitude is due from them to the other

---

* This fact, with his reputed readiness to receive students who had been unsuccessful elsewhere but for whose improvement hope might be entertained, attracted many to him, and filled the higher classes of the institution. One of the leading educators of the country has lately remarked that while this course subjected him to criticism, and might be regarded in some respects with disfavor, it still resulted beneficially, not only to many individuals, but also in rendering college discipline everywhere more parental and inter-collegiate comity more humane. In that day practical efficiency in affairs was most needed for the development of the country; but now, while this is still important, it is felt that thorough training, mental discipline, and complete scholarly furnishing is no less essential to the college graduate. Hence the present aim of Union College is to elevate constantly the standard of scholarship, and with this result in view to secure a well prepared and numerous freshman class. It is found that by an ample and varied course of study, accompanied by rigorous examinations, numbers are much reduced as the class once entered advances from year to year. While this enables individuals who find themselves unfitted for collegiate or professional life to retire without dishonor, and with advantage to themselves and their fellows, those who attain a regular graduation and degree are, it is believed, well fitted for those needs and circumstances of the times which distinguish the present and future from earlier years of national progress. Thus, while stricter examinations tend to decrease the numbers as classes advance, a higher standard of entrance prevents the higher classes from receiving such large accessions from other institutions as were formerly customary. The lower classes, therefore, will be the largest, the base of the pyramid, its broadest part, if the institution is conducted on the system approved by its president as adapted to the present era, enforced heartily by its faculty, and earnestly insisted upon by its alumni and friends, as essential to its reputation, usefulness, and present welfare.

members of the faculty for their talent, fidelity, and ability in conducting the interests more especially confided to their care.*

But advancing age brings its infirmities; and in 1852 the Rev. Laurens P. Hickok, D.D.,† was called from the Auburn

---

*The names of those who have at different periods held a place on the college faculty down to the present time are given in their proper connection in another part of this article; but it will not be invidious to here particularize, in the order of time, those serving ten years or more as tutors or professors:

Rev. Andrew Yates, D.D., (1797-1801, 1814-182-,) professor of Latin and Greek during the first period, and of moral philosophy and logic afterward. He died in Schenectady in 1844.

Rev. Thomas Macauley, D.D., LL.D., (1805-'06, 1811-'22,) tutor, lecturer, and professor of mathematics and natural philosophy. Died in New York in 1862.

Rt. Rev. Thomas C. Brownell, D.D., LL.D., (1805-'19,) successively tutor and professor of logic and belles-lettres, lecturer on chemistry, and professor of rhetoric and chemistry. Afterward Protestant-Episcopal bishop of the diocese of Connecticut till his death at Hartford in 1865.

Pierre Grégoire Reynaud, (1806-'22,) professor of French. Died in Philadelphia, Pa.

Rev. Francis Wayland, (1816-'26,) tutor, and then professor of mathematics and natural philosophy. Afterward president of Brown University. Died in Providence, R. I., in 1865.

Rev. Robert Proudfit, D. D., (1818-'60,) professor of Greek and Latin languages till his death in 1860.

Rt. Rev. Alonzo Potter, D.D., LL.D., (1819-'26, 1831-'45,) tutor, professor of mathematics and natural philosophy, and afterward of rhetoric and natural philosophy. Left college to assume the duties

---

† Dr. Hickok was born in Danbury, Conn., December 29, 1798, graduated at Union College in 1820, and, after serving some years as a pastor, was elected professor of theology in the Western Reserve College. In 1844 he became a professor at Auburn, and in 1866 president of Union College. He resigned this office in 1868 in accordance with a long cherished purpose that at the age of seventy he would retire from active life and devote his time to the revision and extension of his own literary labors, in which he is still engaged. He is residing at Amherst, Mass.

Theological Seminary to serve as vice-president, and upon him gradually devolved the cares of the presidency, although they were not actually conferred in name until after the death of Dr. Nott in 1866.ˈ But in this we are passing over two events of peculiar interest in the history of the college that require a special notice.

SEMI-CENTENNIAL OF UNION COLLEGE.

This event in the history of the college was celebrated in connection with the commencement exercises of 1845, preparations having begun the year before in the appointment of committees and the organization of plans.* The occasion

_____

of Protestant-Episcopal bishop of the diocese of Pennsylvania, and died in California in 1865.

Joel B. Nott, A.M., (1820–'31,) tutor, lecturer, and then professor of chemistry. Now resides in Guilderland, N. Y.

Benjamin F. Joslin, M.D., LL.D., (1822–'37,) tutor, professor of mathematics and natural philosophy. Died in New York in 1861.

Rev. John Austin Yates, D.D., (1823–'49,) tutor, and then professor of Oriental literature till his death in 1849.

Rev. Pierre Alexis Proal, D.D., (1826–'36,) instructor in French. Died in Utica.

Isaac W. Jackson, LL.D., (since 1826,) tutor, and since 1831 professor of mathematics and natural philosophy.

Rev. Thomas C. Reed, D.D., (1826–'51,) tutor, professor of political economy, and afterward of Latin language and literature. Now resides at Geneva, N. Y.

Rev. John Nott, D.D., (1830–'54,) tutor, then assistant professor of rhetoric. Resides in Amsterdam, N. Y.

Jonathan Pearson, A.M., (since 1836,) tutor, assistant professor of

_____

* One man from each of the first twenty classes was designated to this duty, and at the commencement season of 1844 they met to arrange the programme. It was decided that two addresses should be delivered, one from the older and one from the later classes, thus representing, so far as might be, the two epochs of the occasion. The Rev. Jos. Sweetman, of the first class graduated, was chosen for the former, and the Rt. Rev. Alonzo Potter, of the class of 1818, then recently elected Bishop of Penn-

2 U

called together an immense number of the alumni of the college and literary strangers, to receive whom the common
council extended the hospitalities of the city, and all the
principal citizens opened their houses to receive guests. The
proceedings, which extended through several days, were published in a finely printed memorial volume, and left an im-

---

chemistry and natural philosophy, and since 1849 professor of natural
history. Since 1854 he has also filled the office of treasurer.

John Foster, LL.D., (since 1836,) tutor, assistant professor of mathematics and natural philosophy, and since 1849 professor of natural
philosophy.

William Mitchell Gillespie, LL.D., (1845-'68,) professor of civil
engineering and adjunct professor of mathematics. Died in 1868.

Alexander M. Vedder, A.M., M.D., (1849-'63,) professor of anatomy
and physiology.

Tayler Lewis, LL.D., (since 1849,) professor of ancient Oriental
languages and literature.

Elias Peissner, A.M., (1851-'62,) assistant professor of Latin and
teacher of German language and literature, lecturer on political
economy. Was commissioned as colonel of the One hundred and
nineteenth Regiment New York Volunteers, September 1, 1862, and
was killed in battle at Chancellorsville, Va., May 2, 1863.

Rev. John Newman, D.D., (1852-'63,) professor of Latin language
and literature. Now resides in Poultney, Vt.

William Wells, A.M., (since 1865,) professor of modern languages and
literature.

Maurice Perkins, A.M., (since 1865,) professor of chemistry.

Among those of the faculty who held for a short term may be mentioned Mr. Frederick R. Hassler, who, in 1810-'11, held the office of

---

sylvania, but still acting as a professor in the college, was chosen to represent the latter. This selection was eminently fortunate, since no man was
more fully imbued with the spirit of progress or better fitted to represent
the cultured intellect of the living age. Among the names on the committee were the Hon. William H. Seward, Bishop Thomas C. Brownell,
and Hon. Samuel A. Foote, of whom the latter is still living. A tent of
immense size was erected for the dinner, and the tables were set for a
thousand guests.

pression upon the memories of those who participated that would last through life.

SEMI-CENTENNIAL OF DR. NOTT'S PRESIDENCY.

This occasion was celebrated on the 25th of July, 1854, preliminary measures having been taken by the alumni a year before, and the trustees of the college being in full

professor of mathematics and natural philosophy. He became first Superintendent of the United States Coast Survey, and began the precise observations and measurements which have since been continued under his successors, giving this work a just celebrity for accuracy and completeness.

The literary publications of the faculty amount to over sixty in number, and many of them are works of substantial merit.

List of publications by members of the faculty of Union College.

Rev. John Blair Smith, first president of Union College:
  1. The Enlargement of Christ's Kingdom.
  2. A Sermon at Albany. 1767.

Rev. Jonathan Edwards, second president of Union College:
  1. History of the Work of Redemption. Two volumes.
  2. Two volumes of sermons.
  3. Two volumes of observations on important theological subjects

Rev. Eliphalet Nott, fourth president of Union College: —
  1. Counsels to Young Men.
  2. Lectures on Temperance. 1847.
  3. Sermon on the Death of Hamilton. 1804.

Rev. Laurens P. Hickok, fifth president of Union College:
  1. Rational Psychology. 1848.
  2. Moral Science. 1853.
  3. Empirical Psychology. 1854.
  4. Rational Cosmology. 1858.

Rt. Rev. Thomas C. Brownell:
  1. Commentary on the Book of Common Prayer.
  2. Consolation for the Afflicted.
  3. Christian's Walk and Consolation.
  4. Exhortation to Repentance.
  5. Family Prayer-Book.

accord. As on the previous gathering, the hospitalities of the city were tendered to the returning sons of Union and to the literary strangers called together by so unusual an event. The central point of interest was in the address of Dr. Nott, which was a compact review of the labors, joys, and trials of the last fifty years. He might well address to them as a father

---

List of publications, &c.—Continued.

   6. Religion of the Heart and Life. Five volumes.
   7. Religious Enquirer Answered.
   8. Youthful Christian's Guide.

Rev. Francis Wayland:
   1. Moral Dignity of the Missionary Enterprise. 1823.
   2. Duties of an American Citizen. 1825.
   3. Occasional Discourses.
   4. Elements of Moral Science.
   5. Elements of Political Economy. 1837.
   6. Moral Law of Accumulation.
   7. Limitations of Human Responsibility. 1838, and other works.

Rt. Rev. Alonzo Potter:
   1. A Treatise on Logarithms.
   2. A Treatise on Descriptive Geometry.
   3. Political Economy. 1840.
   4. Principles of Science. 1841.
   5. The School and Schoolmaster. [With G. B. Emerson.]
   6. Handbook for Readers and Students. 1843.
   7. Religious Philosophy of Three Witnesses. 1872.

Benjamin F. Joslin:
   1. Homœopathic Treatment of Epidemic Cholera. 1849.
   2. Principles of Homœopathy. 1850, and other publications concerning homœopathy.

Prof. Isaac W. Jackson:
   1. Elements of Conic Sections. 1854.
   2. Elementary Treatise on Optics. 1854.
   3. Elementary Treatise on Mechanics.

Prof. Jonathan Pearson:
   1. Early Records of the City and County of Albany, translated from the Dutch, with notes. 8vo. 1869.

to his children words of counsel, of admonition, and of encouragement; and advice thus given could not fail of making a deep and lasting impression.*

List of publications, &c.—Continued.

2. Contributions for the Genealogies of the First Settlers of the Ancient County of Albany. 1872.
3. Contributions for the Genealogies of the Descendants of the First Settlers of the Town of Schenectady, 1662–1800. 8vo. 1873.

Prof. William M. Gillespie:

1. Rome as Seen by a New Yorker. 1843.
2. Roads and Railroads. 1845.
3. Philosophy of Mathematics, from the French of Comte. 1851.
4. Principles of Land-Surveying. 1855.

Prof. Tayler Lewis:

1. Nature and Ground of Punishment. 1844.
2. Plato contra Atheos. 1845.
3. Six Days of Creation. 1855.
4. Science and the Bible. 1857.

Prof. Elias Peissner:

1. Elements of the German Language. 1854.
2. Elements of the English Language. 1858.
3. Elements of Italian, Spanish, and French, compared with Latin and English. 1859.
4. Course of German and Literature.
5. English Address at the Great Turner Festival, Albany. 1858.
6. The American Question. 1861.

Rev. Robert T. S. Lowell, D.D.:

1. Five Letters to a Romish Priest. 1853.
2. The New Priest in Conception Bay. 1858.
3. Poems. 1860.
4. The Commemoration Hymn for Harvard University Memorial Celebration. 1865.
5. Antony Brade.

---

* The principal orators of the occasion, besides the venerable president, were the Hon. William W. Campbell, of Cherry Valley, and the Rev. Francis Wayland, then president of Brown University. These proceedings were also carefully printed in a collected form.

RECENT HISTORY.

On the retirement of Dr. Hickok, the Rev. Charles A. Aiken, D.D., of Dartmouth College, was chosen president, and he filled the duties with acceptance until 1871, when, for domestic reasons, involving the health of a member of his family, he resigned to seek a less rigorous climate; and in the selection of a successor the choice fell upon the Rev. Eliphalet Nott Potter, D.D., a grandson of Dr. Nott, and son of Bishop Alonzo Potter, already mentioned. This selection of a man at an age much younger than that at which college presidents are usually chosen, might appear to the stranger as a bold departure from established precedent. But the friends of the college justify this action by pointing to the marked improvements since inaugurated, the new buildings erected, the noble endowment funds since received, and the increasing numbers in attendance, especially in the lower classes; and upon these they base their expectations of the future, and look forward with confidence to a new and vigorous growth of the college, with increasing means and a wider field for active usefulness.*

---

* A reference to the accompanying tables will show that the number of students has for several years been steadily increasing, so that the last enrollment in the freshman class was the largest in the history of the college.

It is a matter of history, which our statistics painfully illustrate, that with the declining years of Dr. Nott the number of students decreased, while during the late war the college was nearly stripped of its students by the withdrawal of the whole number from the South, while many from the North were attracted to new institutions that were competing for favor, and appealing to the pride of locality and to various special motives for support. It became a subject of serious thought on the part of those intrusted with the affairs of Union College as to how the emergency was to be met, and no plan appeared more feasible than that of yielding to the progressive spirit of the age, by enlarging its facilities, extending its courses of study, and in the best sense of the word rendering it fully the

PRESENT BUILDINGS.

The principal buildings of Union College are North College and South College, six hundred feet apart, and each with a colonnade facing inward; a Memorial Hall midway between, but standing back three hundred feet from the front line; a gymnasium in the rear of South College; a President's House, and three other dwellings on the line with the main college buildings, and a professor's residence at some distance east of the principal group of buildings.* The original plans con-

peer of the first institutions in the country. The result appears to justify the soundness of this argument, and to encourage persistent and vigorous effort.

*The plans of North and South Colleges are alike except as to the position of the colonnades, and when viewed in front each appears as a pair of large three-story dwellings, connected by a four-story building, the lattei faced with pilasters to the whole height and arches extending up to include the first and second stories. Each college building is 200 by 40 feet on the ground. The end portions are used as residences for professors and the central part as dormitories for students. This central portion has three separate entrances front and rear, with four rooms on each floor, making, originally, forty-eight rooms in each college. Within the past few years a renovation of the interior has been undertaken, and rooms in some cases connected for greater convenience, so as to appear more cheerful and home-like.

The colonnades are each 250 feet in length by 25 in breadth, and terminate in square-roofed buildings one story higher. These buildings are each 80 by 50 feet on the ground. The North Colonnade and building are used for chemical and philosophical apparatus and lecture-rooms, the chemical laboratory and cabinets of the engineering department. Those on the south are used for chapel, library, cabinet, office, and recitation-rooms.

Memorial Hall, so long a familiar object on paper, and originally designed as a chapel, was delayed from various causes, so that its foundations were not laid till 1858, and the effort was then suspended when the walls had reached the level of the first story. Work has been recently resumed by the aid of funds given by two brothers of President Potter, amounting to $50,000, and the work at the time of writing is fully in-

templated two other college edifices to the rear, facing west-
ward upon the campus, with a semicircular connecting colonnade, but it is doubtful whether these intentions will ever be
fully carried out.

PRESENT GROUNDS.

The original grounds acquired for college uses have been
somewhat reduced by railroad and street improvements, but
are scarcely liable to further encroachment, and are amply
sufficient for every probable want.   They embrace about one

---

closed and rapidly approaching completion. The building has sixteen
equal sides, is eighty-four feet in diameter and fifty feet in height to the top
of the walls.   It is surmounted by a dome of corrugated iron, covered with
metal plates, and within plastered for frescoing.   The dome is spangled
with gilded stars and has other appropriate ornamentation.   The walls are
of bluestone, from the vicinity, with white Ohio sandstone trimmings, and
cylindrical columns of polished granite in the windows.   The dome rises
one hundred and twenty feet above the floor, and the interior will form
one spacious rotunda, with galleries and alcoves for the library, and an
appropriate repository for works of art.

The gymnasium was completed in 1874, at the cost of prominent alumni
of Albany and Troy, and through the efforts of students in gathering
subscriptions, and is one of the largest and best equipped establishments
of the kind in the country.   It is under the control of a professional
gymnast, whose theory is to use its peculiar opportunities for physical
development and manly exercise, to the exclusion of all useless and dan-
gerous feats.   The building is 80 by 40 feet on the ground, and two stories
in height.

The President's House was built in 1873, chiefly from the donation to
the Christian Union endowment-fund by a member of the board of trustees,
and its style is in harmony with the general plan.

A cottage in the Swiss style of architecture was built in the gardens
north of North College in 1873, and from its fine location, half concealed
by trees, it presents a picturesque appearance from favorable points of
view.

All of these buildings, except memorial hall and the cottage, are of
brick, rough-cast with ash-colored cement, with pilasters, arches, and
trimmings in white, presenting a general unity of plan and symmetry of
proportion that is quite pleasing in general effect.

hundred and thirty acres, including the campus, gardens, and grounds properly belonging to the college and essential for its use, besides some one hundred acres of woodlands and fields adjoining.

THE JACKSON GARDEN.

During the residence of Prof. Thomas Macauley, more than fifty years ago, a beginning was made in the improvement of a garden north of North College. The work was, however, scarcely more than a beginning until Prof. Isaac W. Jackson became a resident of the adjoining dwelling in 1831, when a series of improvements were begun, which, aided by a small annual grant from the trustees, have gradually transformed a wild ravine and tangled woodland into a charming ramble and pleasant retreat. The grounds embrace some twelve acres, and combine many attractions of sylvan solitude and floral beauty.*

COURSE OF STUDY.

The details of the course of study first established in Union College cannot be determined with certainty from existing records, but the curriculum of 1802 will be found in the following table. We also ·give the course of study at nearly even decennial periods, so far as the data at hand will permit.

---

* By the act of 1814 giving to Columbia College the title to the botanical gardens, that have since formed so noble a source of wealth, it was provided that within one year at least one healthy exotic flower, shrub, or plant of each kind in duplicate, with the jar containing it, should be sent, if applied for, to each other college in the State. There is not found any record showing that any plants were received by Union College under this act.

Classical course of study in Union

	1802.	1833.	1844.
FRESHMAN YEAR. *First term.*	"The Freshman class shall study the Latin, Greek, and English Languages, Arithmetic, Sheridan's Lectures on Elocution, and shall write such Latin exercises as the Faculty may appoint."	Cicero de Officiis, de Amicitia, &c. Horace and Latin Prosody, with composition and declamation. Herodotus and Thucydides.	Livy. Horace and Latin Prosody, with composition and declamation. Xenophon's Anabasis.
Second term.		Xenophon's Cyropædia and Anabasis. Horace, Roman Antiquities. Livy, with composition and declamation.	Herodotus and Thucydides. Horace, Roman Antiquities. Algebra to Chapter III, (Bourdon.)
Third term.		Sallust. Algebra, (through equations of the first degree.) Lysias, Isocrates, and Demosthenes, with composition and declamation.	Cicero de Officiis, with composition and declamation. Algebra, (continued.) Lysias, Isocrates, and Demosthenes.
SOPHOMORE YEAR. *First term.*	"The Sophomore class shall study Geography, Algebra, Vulgar and Decimal Fractions, the Extraction of Roots, Conic Sections, Euclid's Elements, Trigonometry, Surveying, Mensuration of Heights and Distances, Navigation, Logic, Blair's Lectures, and such parts of eminent authors in the learned languages as the officers in college shall prescribe."	Tacitus' History. Xenophon's Memorabilia and Plato. Algebra, (continued.)	Tacitus' History; Geology twice a week. Xenophon's Memorabilia. Plane Geometry.
Second term.		Aristotle, Dyonisius, and Longinus. Tacitus, (continued.) Plane Geometry.	Greek Majora. Juvenal and Terence. Solid Geometry.
Third term.		Homer's Odyssey. Solid Geometry. Logic.	Homer's Iliad. Trigonometry. Abercrombie's Intellectual Powers; Botany, (twice a week.)

College at different periods.

1854.	1864.	1875.
Livy, 3 books. Xenophon's Anabasis, 2 books. Algebra, to Square Root.	Livy, 3 books. Xenophon's Cyropædia. Algebra, to "Series."	Livy. Xenophon; Homer. Algebra—(continued)—to "Series." Greek prose composition. Latin prose composition.
Horace, 3 books of Odes; Prosody. Demosthenes' Philippics. Algebra, (to *n*th root.)	Horace, 3 books of Odes; Prosody. Xenophon's Memorabilia. Algebra, (completed.)	Horace. Xenophon; Homer; Herodotus. Algebra, completed. Greek prose composition. Latin prose composition.
Cicero de Officiis, 2 books. Homer's Iliad, 4 books. Geometry, Plane, 5 books.	Cicero de Officiis, 2 books. Homer. Iliad, 4 books. Geometry, Plane, 5 books.	Cicero de Senectute and de Amicitia. Xenophon; Herodotus; Euripides. Geometry, Books VI to IX. Trigonometry. Rhetoric, with composition and declamation. Greek prose composition. Latin prose composition.
(Throughout Freshman year, exercises in Latin and Greek composition.)	*(Throughout Freshman year, exercises in Latin and Greek composition.)*	*(Physical culture 3 hours a week, and English composition throughout the year.)*
Tacitus' History, 2 books, or Germania and Agricola. Homer, Odyssey, 6 books. Geometry, Solid, 4 books.	Tacitus' History, 2 books, or Germania and Agricola. Homer, Odyssey, 6 books. Geometry, Solid, 4 books. Rhetoric.	Tacitus. Euripides; Æschylus. History of the United States. Rhetoric, Art of Discourse. Review of freshman mathematics.
Juvenal, (1st and 10th;) Terence, (one.) Xenophon's Memorabilia, 3 books. Algebra, (completed.)	Juvenal, (1st, 3d, and 10th;) Terence, (one.) Euripides, one or two Dramas. Algebra, (completed.) Study of Words.	Juvenal and Terence. Euripides; Æschylus. Conic Sections. Logic.
Logic. Euripides, one or two Dramas. Trigonometry, Plane and Spherical. Horace, Satires and Epistles, (voluntary.)	Horace, Satires and Epistles. Sophocles, 2 Dramas. Trigonometry, Plane and Spherical.	Horace, Satires and Epistles. Euripides; Sophocles; Plato. Statics and Dynamics. Study of Man. Botany, (voluntary.) History.
	(Throughout Sophomore year, exercises in translating Greek into Latin.)	*(Physical culture 3 hours a week, and composition and declamation throughout the year.)*

Classical course of study in Union Col

		1802.	1833.	1844.
JUNIOR YEAR.	*First term.*	"The Junior class shall study the Elements of Criticism, Astronomy, Natural and Moral Philosophy, and shall perform such exercises in the higher branches of the Mathematics as the Faculty shall prescribe."	Trigonometry and Applications. Hesiod and Sophocles. Rhetoric.	Conic Sections. Hesiod and Sophocles. Rhetoric. Heeren's Ancient Greece, (twice a week.)
	Second term.		Cicero de Oratore. Conic Sections. Natural Philosophy, (statics.)	Cicero de Oratore, or Plautus. Chemistry. Natural Philosophy, (statics.) Heeren's Greece, (completed.)
	Third term.		Political Economy. Medea, &c. Natural Philosophy, Dynamics, Hydrostatics, &c.	Political Economy. Medea, &c. Natural Philosophy, Dynamics, Hydrostatics, &c. Technology.

lege at different periods—Continued.

1854.	1864.	1875.
Cicero, Tusculan Questions, 3 books. Rhetoric. Conic Sections, (Jackson's,) or Analytical Geometry.	Cicero, Tusculan Questions, 3 books. Æschylus, 2 Dramas. Conic Sections, (Jackson's,) or Analytical Geometry. English Language. Chemistry, (inorganic.)	Cicero, Tusculan Disputations. Sophocles; Æschylus; Thucydides. Mechanical Work—Hydrostatics, Hydrodynamics, Pneumatics. Elocution. Political Economy.
Chemistry. Sophocles, 2 Dramas. Statics and Dynamics.	Quintilian. Plato, Phædon or Gorgias. Rhetoric. Chemistry, (organic.)	Lucretius or Quintilian. Plato ; Demosthenes. Elocution. Heat: Steam-engine; Electricity ; Meteorology. Physiology. Ethics.
Political Economy. Plato, Phædon or Gorgias. Hydrostatics; Hydrodynamics; Pneumatics; Heat ; Steam.	Statics and Dynamics. Geology. Physiology.	Acoustics ; Magnetism ; Galvanism; Electro-Magnetism. Chemistry. History of Civilization. Zoölogy. Botany. (*Composition and declamation and physical culture 3 hours a week throughout the year.*)

Classical course of study in Union Col

		1802.*	1833.	1844.
SENIOR YEAR.	First term.	"The Senior class shall study select portions of Ancient and Modern History, such parts of Locke's Essay on the Human Understanding as the President shall direct, Stewart's Elements of the Philosophy of the Human Mind, and shall review the principal studies of the preceding years, and also such portions of Virgil, Cicero, and Horace as the President shall direct, and shall be accustomed to apply the principles of criticism."	Intellectual Philosophy. Lectures on Electricity, and Biot's Optics. Elements of Criticism.	Moral Philosophy. Astronomy and Lectures on Electricity. Technology, (completed.) Elements of Criticism.
	Second term.		Astronomy. Moral Philosophy. Kames, and Lectures on Chemistry.	Optics. Psychology. Kames, and Michelet's History. Lectures on Magnetism, Galvanism, and Electro-Magnetism.
	Third term.		Hebrew. Greek Testament, with Lectures on Biblical Literature. Lectures on Elements of Criticism, Chemistry, Botany, and Mineralogy.	Hebrew, with Lectures on Biblical Literature. Guizot's History of Civilization. Butler's Analogy, (twice a week.) Botany, Geology, and Mineralogy. Anatomy and Physiology, (3 times a week.) Synoptical view of the Sciences, in Lectures. *(Lectures are also delivered during the course on Natural Philosophy, Rhetoric and Oratory, Political Economy, Metaphysical and Moral Philosophy, and the Philosophy of History.)*

* The statutes of 1802 prescribe, besides the course of studies given in the table,
The freshmen and sophomores shall recite three times each day, in term-time,
ter vacation, and twice each day after the winter vacation until commencement.
time each day until their final examination.
The sophomores, juniors, and seniors shall exhibit compositions of their own, in
time for this purpose, the recitation on Fridays in the afternoon shall be omitted.
indecent, profane, or immoral.

ege at different periods—Continued.

1854.	1864.	1875.
Optics. Sound; Electricity; Magnetism; Galvanism; Electro-Magnetism. Mental Philosophy. Criticism. Plato contra Atheos, (voluntary.)	Plato contra Atheos,(voluntary.) Hydrostatics; Hydrodynamics: Pneumatics; Heat; Steam. Optics. Mental Philosophy Lectures on History of Philosophy.	Optics; Wave Theory of Light and Radiant Heat. Mental Philosophy. Lectures on Greek Philosophy. Geology. Plato contra Atheos, (voluntary.) Applied Chemistry. Chemical Laboratory exercises.
Astronomy. Aristophanes, Birds or Clouds. Moral Philosophy. Criticism.	Aristophanes, Birds or Clouds, (voluntary.) Sound; Electricity; Magnetism; Galvanism; Electro-Magnetism. Astronomy. Moral Philosophy. Lectures on Ancient Poetry.	Astronomy. Ethics. Christian Evidences. Lectures on Greek Philosophy and Poetry. Aristophanes, Birds or Clouds, (voluntary.) Hebrew, (voluntary.) English Literature. Lectures on the Bible. Comparative Philology.
National and Constitutional Law. Anatomy and Physiology, (Lectures.) Moral Philosophy. Lectures on Classical and Modern Literature, Architecture, &c.	History of Philosophy. Principles of Eloquence. English Literature; Lectures. Agricultural Chemistry and Geology. Lectures on Biblical Literature, Architecture, &c.	Christian Ethics. International Law and Constitution of the United States. Lectures on English Poetry. Lectures on English Literature. Lectures on Biblical Literature. Lectures on Greek Poetry. Lectures on Art. Lectures on History. Mineralogy, (voluntary.)
	(Rhetorical exercises by Seniors, Juniors, and Sophomores before the whole College, in the Chapel, on Saturdays, at 8 a. m.)	*(Physical culture 3 hours a week, and rhetorical exercises throughout the year.)*

the following requirements:
during the year. The junior three times each day, until the beginning of the winter
The seniors shall recite twice each day until the winter vacation, and from that

the English language, every Saturday morning. That they may have sufficient
Every student is strictly forbidden to exhibit anything in his compositions that

Scientific course of study in Union

	1833.	1844.
FRESHMAN YEAR. *First term.*	[Same as in Classical Course.]	[Same as in Classical Course.]
Second term.	[Same as in Classical Course.]	[Same as in Classical Course.]
Third term.	[Same as in Classical Course.]	[Same as in Classical Course.]
SOPHOMORE YEAR. *First term.*	History. Arithmetic. Algebra, (continued.)	Tacitus ; Geology. History. Plane Geometry.
Second term.	History, (continued.) Natural Theology. Plane Geometry.	Natural Theology. Juvenal and Terence. Solid Geometry.
Third term.	Natural History. Solid Geometry. Logic.	Natural History. Trigonometry and Applications. Abercrombie's Intellectual Powers, and Botany.

College at different periods.

1854.	1864.	1875.
[Same as in Classical Course.]	[Same as in Classical Course.]	Latin Grammar and Reader. French Grammar. Algebra — (continued) — to "Series." History.
[Same as in Classical Course.]	[Same as in Classical Course.]	Latin Grammar and Reader. French Grammar and Reader. Algebra, (completed.)
[Same as in Classical Course.]	[Same as in Classical Course.]	French Grammar and Reader. Geometry, Books VI to IX. Rhetoric, with composition and declamation. Trigonometry. (*Physical culture 3 hours a week and English composition throughout the year.*)
French. History. Geometry, Solid, 4 books.	French, (Grammar.) History. Geometry, Solid, four books. Rhetoric.	French Classic Poetry. German Grammar. Descriptive Geometry. History of the United States. Rhetoric; Art of Discourse. Review of freshman mathematics.
French, (continued.) Draughting. Algebra, (completed.)	French, (Reader.) Geometrical Draughting. Algebra, (completed.) Study of Words.	Contemporary French Literature. German Grammar. Conic Sections. Logic. Ancient History, eclectic. Mensuration, eclectic. Descriptive Geometry, eclectic.
Logic. Land-Surveying. Trigonometry, Plane and Spherical. Descriptive Geometry, (voluntary.) Italian, (voluntary.)	Trigonometry, Plane and Spherical. Land-Surveying, (Parts 1, 2, 3.) Draughting, (voluntary.) French, (Molière or Racine.) Italian, (voluntary.) Botany, (voluntary.)	Contemporaneous French Literature. German Grammar and Reader. Statics and Dynamics. Study of Man. Botany, (voluntary.) Analytical Geometry, eclectic. Surveying, eclectic. (*Physical culture 3 times a week: English composition and declamation throughout the year.*)

3 U

Scientific course of study in Union Col

		1833.	1844.
JUNIOR YEAR.	*First term.*	Trigonometry and Applications. Algebra. Rhetoric.	Conic Sections. Algebra. Rhetoric. Heeren's Ancient Greece, (twice a week.)
	Second term.	French. Descriptive Geometry; Analytical Geometry of two Dimensions. Natural Philosophy, (Statics.)	German. Chemistry. Natural Philosophy, (Statics.) Heeren's Greece, (completed.) Topography, (extra study.)
	Third term.	Differential and Integral Calculus. Analytical Geometry of three Dimensions. Natural Philosophy, (Dynamics, Hydrostatics, &c.)	Differential and Integral Calculus. Analytical Geometry of three Dimensions. Natural Philosophy—Dynamics, Hydrostatics, &c. Technology. French, (extra study.) Surveying and Leveling, (extra study.)

lege at different periods—Continued.

1854.	1864.	1875.
German. Rhetoric. Conic Sections, (Jackson's,) or Analytical Geometry. Draughting, (continued,) (voluntary,) Lectures. Leveling, (voluntary,) Lectures.	German, (Grammar.) Analytical Geometry. Descriptive Geometry. English Language. Chemistry, (Inorganic.)	German Literature. Mechanical Work; Hydrostatics; Hydrodynamics; Pneumatics. Political Economy. Elocution. Drawing.
Chemistry. German, (continued.) Statics and Dynamics. Differential and Integral Calculus, (voluntary.) Draughting, (continued,) (voluntary.) Engineering; Mensuration, (voluntary.) Applied Mechanics, (voluntary.)	German, (Reader.) Rhetoric. Chemistry, (Organic.) Differential and Integral Calculus, (voluntary.) Draughting, (continued,) (voluntary.)	German Literature. Elocution. Heat; Steam-engine; Electricity; Meteorology. Physiology. Ethics.
Political Economy. German, (continued.) Hydrostatics; Hydrodynamics; Pneumatics; Heat; Steam. Analytical Mechanics, (voluntary.) Higher Surveying, (voluntary,) Lectures. Strength of Materials, (voluntary,) Lectures. Applied Mechanics, (voluntary,) Lectures. Botany, (voluntary.)	Statics and Dynamics. Geology. Mineralogy, (Determinative), (voluntary.) Analytical Mechanics, (voluntary.) Draughting, (continued,) (voluntary.) German, (Literature,) (voluntary.) Physiology.	Acoustics; Magnetism; Galvanism; Electro-magnetism. Chemistry. Zoölogy. History of Civilization. Botany, (voluntary.) *(Physical culture 3 times a week, and composition and declamation throughout the year.)*

Scientific course of study in Union Col

	1833.	1844.
SENIOR YEAR. *First term.*	Boucharlat's Mechanics. Lectures on Electricity and Magnetism, and Biot's Optics. Elements of Criticism.	Boucharlat's Mechanics. Astronomy, and Lectures on Electricity. Technology. Elements of Criticism. Topography and Practical Astronomy.
Second term.	Moral Philosophy. Astronomy. Kames, and Lectures on Chemistry.	Optics. Psychology. Kames and Michelet. Prometheus Vinctus of Æschylus, to an extra division.
Third term.	Law, (Kent or Blackstone.) Anatomy and Physiology. Lectures on Elements of Criticism, Chemistry, Botany, and Mineralogy.	Law. Michelet. Butler's Analogy, (twice a week.) Botany, Geology, and Mineralogy. Anatomy and Physiology, (three times a week.) Synoptical view of the Sciences, in Lectures. *(A lecture is also delivered each Sunday evening on the Evidences of Christianity, or on some portion of Scripture.)*

*lege at different periods—*Concluded.

1854.	1864.	1875.
Optics. Sound; Electricity; Magnetism; Galvanism; Electro-Magnetism. Mental Philosophy. Criticism. Roads and Railroads,(voluntary.) Engineering, Field Work, (voluntary.) Stability of Structures, (voluntary,) Lectures. Geology, (voluntary.)	Hydrostatics; Hydrodynamics; Pneumatics; Heat; Steam. Optics. Mental Philosophy. Surveying (continued) and Leveling, (voluntary.)	Optics; Wave Theory of Light and Radiant Heat. Mental Philosophy. Applied Chemistry. Chemical Laboratory Exercises. Geology.
Astronomy. Spanish. Moral Philosophy. Criticism. Engineering Construction, (voluntary.) Bridges, (voluntary,) Lectures. Hydraulic Engineering, (voluntary,) Lectures.	Sound; Electricity; Magnetism; Galvanism; Electro-Magnetism. Astronomy. Moral Philosophy. Spanish, (voluntary.) Engineering, Mensuration, &c., (voluntary,) Lectures.	Astronomy. Ethics. Christian Evidences. Lectures on English Literature. Lectures on the Bible. Physical Laboratory Exercises.
National and Constitutional Law. Anatomy and Physiology, (Lectures.) Moral Philosophy. Geodosy and Practical Astronomy, (voluntary.) Architecture, (voluntary,) Lectures.	History of Philosophy. Lectures on Biblical Literature, Architecture, &c. Principles of Eloquence. English Literature, Lectures. Agricultural Chemistry and Geology. Higher Surveying and Engineering Statics, (voluntary.)	Christian Ethics. International Law and Constitution of the United States. Lectures on English Poetry. Lectures on Biblical Literature. Higher Surveying and Engineering Statics, (voluntary.) Mineralogy, (voluntary.) Lectures on Art. Lectures on English Literature. Lectures on History.
	(Rhetorical exercises by Seniors, Juniors, and Sophomores before the whole College, in Chapel, on Saturdays at 8 a. m.)	*(Physical culture 3 hours a week, and rhetorical exercises throughout the year.)*

DEPARTMENT OF CIVIL ENGINEERING.

This was established in 1845, under the direction of Prof. William M. Gillespie;* its course of instruction aiming to impart skill and experience in mechanical draughting, instrumental field-work, and numerical calculation, combined with the study of text-books and lectures on numerous subjects where these are wanting. The canal, with its extensive aqueducts; the various railroads centering in Schenectady, with their numerous bridges and other structures, and extensive locomotive works, founderies, shops, and factories, afford a fine opportunity for examination and study in this department. This course has recently been extended to four years, and intermingled with the scientific course of the college proper. The student thus gains a knowledge of modern languages so essential to the civil engineer, and the advantage of that mental discipline that tends largely to success in life. The department is well supplied with models, the most important of which is the Olivier collection.†

---

* Professor Gillespie, who was distinguished alike as a teacher and an author in the special lines of his study, died in New York, January 1, 1868.

† This consists of about fifty models, representing the most important and complicated ruled surfaces of descriptive geometry, particularly warped or twisted surfaces. Their directrices are represented by brass bars, straight or curved, to which are attached silk threads representing the elements or successive positions of the generatrices of the surfaces. Each of these threads has a weight suspended by it so as always to make it a straight line. These weights are contained in boxes sustaining the directrices and their standards. The bars are movable in various directions, carrying with them the threads still stretched straight by the weights in every position they may take; so that the forms and natures of the surfaces which they constitute are continually changing, while they always remain "ruled surfaces." In this way a plane is transformed into a paraboloid, a cylinder into a hyperboloid, &c. These models were invented by the lamented Théodore Olivier, while professor of descriptive geometry

CHEMICAL LABORATORY.

A laboratory was established for chemical analysis in 1855 at a cost of about $7,000 for fixtures and $10,000 for chemicals and other stock. It has been successively in charge of Professors Charles E. Joy and Charles F. Chandler, (now both of Columbia College,) and of Maurice Perkins, M.D., the present incumbent. It has working facilities for twenty students, and fifteen are now attending.

COURSE OF STUDIES IN THE ENGINEERING DEPARTMENT, UNION COLLEGE, 1875.

FRESHMAN CLASS.

First term.—Latin—French grammar—Algebra (continued) to "Series"—Drawing.

Second term.—Latin—French grammar and reader—Algebra, (completed)—Drawing, plane problems.

Third term.—English language—French grammar and reader—Geometry, books VI to IX—Trigonometry, plane and spherical—Calculations; rapid, accurate, and approximate.

(Physical culture three hours a week and English composition throughout the year.)

---

at the Conservatoire des Arts et Métiers, in Paris. One set of them is now deposited there, and a second is in the Conservatory of Madrid. Copies of some of them are to be found in most of the polytechnic schools of Germany. The Union College set is the original collection of the inventor, having been made in part by his own hands, and after his death in 1853, retained by his widow till bought from her by Professor Gillespie, in 1855. It is more complete than that in the Paris Conservatoire. It may be worth noticing that the silvered plates on the boxes, reading " *Inventé par Théodore Olivier*," &c., were added by Madame Olivier after the purchase, at her own expense, as a tribute to the memory of her husband; her own words being " *Je tenais à ce que chaque instrument portât le nom du savant dont la réputation passera à la postérité.*"

SOPHOMORE CLASS.

First term.—French poetry—German grammar—Descriptive geometry—Rhetoric—History of thè United States—Review of freshman mathematics.

Second term.—Contemporaneous French literature—German grammar and reader—Conic sections—Descriptive geometry—Mensuration—Logic—Drawing, shades and shadows.

Third term.—Contemporaneous French literature—German grammar and reader—Statics and dynamics—Surveying—Analytical geometry—Study of man—History.

(Physical culture three hours a week and English composition throughout the year.)

JUNIOR CLASS.

First term.—German literature—Hydrostatics, hydrodynamics and pneumatics—Surveying—Machines—Political economy.

Second term.—German literature—Electricity, magnetism, galvanism—Physiology—Calculus—Drawing, oblique proection.

Third term.—Chemistry—Heat, steam-engine—Strength of materials—Zoölogy—Topographical mapping.

(Physical culture three hours a week and composition and declamation throughout the year.)

SENIOR CLASS.

First term.—Road engineering—Geology—Optics—Chemistry—Stability of structures.

Second term.—Engineering construction—Astronomy—Metallurgy—Ethics—Drawing.

·*Third term.*—Physical Laboratory—Physical geography—

Moral philosophy—Law of contracts and right of way—
Botany—Thesis.

(Throughout the year, physical culture three hours a week
and rhetorical exercises.)

MILITARY INSTRUCTION.

In 1873 Union College applied to the War Department,
requesting that an officer of the Engineer Corps might be de-
tailed for the purpose of giving military instruction, in pursuance of the policy favored by act of Congress, with the
view of inducing colleges to supplement in some degree the
work of the military academy in this department of useful
knowledge.   The Government has, in accordance with this
request, supplied the college with muskets and equipments
for drill and instruction, under a commissioned officer of the
Army.   A plain, inexpensive uniform has been adopted,
and a course of military instruction has been added to the
college curriculum without abating anything from the course
of studies formerly prescribed.   The drill is regarded chiefly
as a physical training.   Capt. Thomas Ward of Second Ar-
tillery, U.S.A., is the present military instructor.

COLLEGE SOCIETIES.

Union College has at present two literary societies with
libraries,* a theological society,† societies for practice in par-

---

* The Philomathean Society was formed in 1793 by young men in town,
at the old academy, before a college charter was granted.   It was first called
the "Calliopean," and it held its first meeting under its present name in
October, 1795.   It celebrated its semi-centennial (somewhat behind time)
in 1848.   Its hall is in the upper story of the south dwelling of South
College, and it possesses a library of about three thousand volumes.

The Adelphic Society was founded in 1797, and celebrated its semi-

---

† Formed in 1831 for discussion of moral and religious subjects.

liamentary debate,* seven "Greek letter" societies,† and a
chapter of the Phi Beta Kappa Society.‡

An alumni association was formed in 1857, and has
several branches.§

---

centennial in 1848. Its hall is in the upper story of the north dwelling of
North College, and its library contains about three thousand volumes.

The Delphian Institute, originally formed in 1819, by students from
the South, was limited in membership to thirty-six. In 1848 it was
merged into the Adelphic. Its hall was in the upper story of the south
dwelling of North College.

* A "senate" and a "house of representatives" were formed for pur-
poses of debate on political subjects, the former consisting of the senior
and the latter of the junior class. The rules of order and method of
procedure are modeled, as near as may be, after those of the Senate and
House of Representatives of the United States.

† These societies in the order of establishment here have been K. A.,
Kappa Alpha, 1825; Σ. Φ., Sigma Phi, 1827; Δ. Φ., Delta Phi, 1827;
Ψ. Υ., Psi Upsilon, 1833; Δ. Υ., Delta Upsilon, 1834; X. Ψ., Chi Psi,
1841; Θ. Δ. X , Theta Delta Chi, 1847, (not now in existence here;)
Fraternal Society, O. K. E., 1834, (united with A. Δ. Φ. ;) O. A. or
Equitable Union, 1837; Z. Ψ., Zeta Psi, 1856. (discontinued here;) Δ.
K. E., Delta Kappa Epsilon, 1857, (discontinued here;) A. Δ. Φ., Alpha
Delta Phi, 1859; and Σ. T., Sigma Tau, 1872.

‡ The Alpha Chapter, Φ. B. K, of the State of New York, was established at this college in 1817, and is a strictly honorary society.

§ The general catalogues of Union College contain a list of names of
which the college and the country may be proud. Upon these dependence
might be safely placed in whatever concerns her interests, and accordingly a modification of the charter was procured in 1871, by granting to
them a representation in the board of trustees, so that now there are four
graduates holding this trust, one being chosen annually for a term of
four years. The elections are held on alumni day, the one preceding
commencement, in the chapel, at Schenectady. Prof. William Wells
has, for several years, taken an active interest in this movement. He
has recently visited many points in the country, at which the graduates
of Union College might be assembled, and with gratifying results.

SCHOLARSHIPS.

Under an act passed in 1814, the sum of fifty thousand dollars was set apart as a fund, the income of which has ever since been applied in aiding young men of narrow means, and thus multitudes have gone out into active life well prepared, who but for this would have failed to receive a thorough education. This aid is granted without reference to the intended profession, and with the sole object of accomplishing the greatest good. It is believed that the number thus needing encouragement has relatively increased since the war, and that the sons of rich men now seek immediate opportunities for business, without waiting for that preparation by way of college training that was formerly deemed requisite. The great number of fortunes hastily made within a few years, has attracted the notice and stimulated the ambition of many who have yet to learn from experience that such fortunes may be speedily lost. This tendency appears to impose the necessity of aiding those of the less fortunate class, but who, from the increasing cost of subsistence and personal expenses, are finding it annually more difficult to overcome these obstacles without pecuniary aid. The endowment of funds for this object becomes, therefore, a philanthropic duty, and it is with peculiar satisfaction that the officers of the college are able to acknowledge the receipt of several noble benefactions for this object, with assurances of more.*

---

*Actuated by this spirit, Miss Catharine L. Wolfe, of New York City, in 1873, informed President Potter of an intention of giving fifty thousand dollars, in pursuance of a purpose entertained by her deceased father, Mr. John David Wolfe, for the purpose of aiding the education of young men from the Southern States. The father having died before this plan was matured, the sum above mentioned has since been paid in by the daughter and securely invested at 7 per cent. for this object. Already some-

An effort is being made to introduce the system of en-
couraging students to regard the sums released to them, and
other aid received from relief funds, as loans to be returned
after leaving college, and as soon as they can conveniently re-
pay them from their own earnings. This would tend to encourage a spirit of independence, and the student would
feel himself no longer an object of charity, but rather
one trusted upon his honor, on account of his talents and
moral worth. The idea that a student can maintain himself
by his own labor while pursuing his studies, is not entertained
in this college. If it has succeeded in some cases these are
exceptional to the general rule. If self-support must accom-
pany the effort to gain an education, it can only be by alternate study and labor, a course sometimes attended with the
advantage of enabling the student to apply the precepts of
his college studies. It more generally, however, delays preparation for life's duties, and often leads to the abandonment
of a course before it is completed.

I. ORDINARY SCHOLARSHIPS.—To a large class of students,
Union College presents extraordinary advantages in its
numerous scholarships. In the scholarships of the first
grade, the incumbents, on the condition of good conduct
and satisfactory application to study, receive at the end of

---

twenty-five Southern students, mainly from the excellent preparatory institution at Charleston, S. C., established and maintained by the Rev. A·
Tamor Porter, are enjoying this benefaction.

A recent bequest of nearly fifty thousand dollars, by Dr. John Mc-
Clelland, of New York City, of the class of 1832, has also been made.
He was largely influenced in this by the aid he had himself received while
in college.

Still more recently it has been learned that a worthy son of Union
College has placed a bequest of thirty thousand dollars in his will, to en-
dow an emeritus professorship, in gratitude for generous aid in his youthful struggles for an education.

each term a credit on the books of the registrar, to the full amount of the term-bill.

In the scholarships of the second grade, the incumbents, on the same condition, receive a credit to the amount of half the term-bill.

These scholarships are accessible, under certain restrictions, to all who present the requisite certificates of character and sustain the examinations required for admission to the regular classes of the college.

II. PRIZE SCHOLARSHIPS.—Among the several classes of scholarships founded by the late Dr. Eliphalet Nott,* is a class of prize scholarships.

An examination of candidates for these scholarships is held early in the first term of the freshman year, and also at a later period in the same year, and the appointments are made according to certain rules prescribed by the founder.

The pecuniary emolument of a prize scholarship is thirty-five dollars a term, or four hundred and twenty dollars for the whole college course, a provision which enables the incumbent, after paying his college bills, to retain the sum of one hundred and twenty dollars.

The possession of a prize scholarship being a special distinction, the incumbent is expected and required to maintain, throughout his whole course, high standing as a student in all respects.

Among the rules which the incumbent is required to observe is one which forbids the use, during the period of incumbency, of intoxicating liquor as a beverage and of tobacco in all its forms.

---

*Few of these are yet actually endowed, but their ultimate endowment is secured by the prospective sale of valuable lands.

Some of the scholarships enable the student to pursue post-graduate studies for a certain time, but of fellowships, properly so-called, the college has none.

III. Prizes and Medals.—The following prizes have been established in Union College:

Name.	Princi-pal.	Annual value.	Object and remarks.
1 Blatchford Orato-rical Medals.—(By the late Richard M. Blatchford, of New York.)	$1,000	$40 and $30..	For first and second grade of merit in oratory, " regard being had alike to their elevated and classical character, and to their graceful and effective deliv-ery."
2. Warner Prize.—(By Hon. Horatio G. Warner, of Ro-chester.)	714	$50 in money or plate.	To the graduate of the classical course standing highest in the performance of college duties, and sustaining the best charac-ter for moral rectitude and de-portment, without regard to religious profession or practice.
3. Ingham Prize.—(By Hon. Albert C. Ing-ham, of Meridian, N. Y.)	1,000	$70 in money or plate.	To a graduate (of at least two years' residence) for the best essay on one of two subjects, previously assigned, in English literature or history.

IV. Prize Essays.—Prizes are awarded to the two mem-bers of the senior class who present the best essays on English literature, on subjects assigned the previous term.

V. Prize Speaking.—Prizes are awarded to the two members of the junior and sophomore classes, respectively, who deliver the best orations on the occasion of prize speak-ing during commencement week. Six juniors and four sophomores are selected for this exercise; regard being had both to composition and to delivery.

The prizes are in the form of valuable books, and are announced at commencement.

VI. Special Prize.—The inaugural prize, established by the president at his inauguration, is assigned from year to year under such conditions as may be previously announced.

COLLEGE LIBRARIES.

There are three libraries connected with the institution, of which the college library proper contains about twelve thousand volumes, the Philomathean Society library three thousand, and the Adelphic three thousand volumes.*

COLLECTIONS IN NATURAL HISTORY.

From an early period the college has been a center of interest for students of natural history, and collections were added from time to time, especially in 1841, when a considerable number of minerals and fossils were received from the State cabinet. In 1860 the "Wheatley collection" of shells and minerals, valued at the time as worth $20,000, and now still more, was presented by Mr. E. C. Delavan.

The dredgings upon our coast in recent years have enriched the cabinet with many forms of marine life, and within the last three years an extensive collection of specimens was added by Prof. H. E. Webster as the result of his labors in dredging at Eastport, Me., on the coast of Massachusetts and Virginia, and the west coast of Florida.

A valuable herbarium has been given by Dr. George T. Stevens, of Albany.

PHILOSOPHICAL DEPARTMENT.

In this department the collections, under the care of Prof. John Foster, have grown to be among the finest in the country. The donations of friends have added largely to their value,† but the principal part has been purchased by the friends of the college or by special funds raised for this pur-

---

* In 1873 Mr. James Brown, of New York, gave the sum of $10,000, under the name of the "Coe memorial fund." The income is applied to increasing the college library, which it does at the rate of about two hundred volumes a year.

† The donors to this department are William H. H. Moore, Hon. A. H. Rice, Henry C. Potter, M.D., Henry R. Pierson, Howard Potter, William A. Whitbeck, C. N. Potter, Lemon Thomson, and A. Q. Stevens.

pose. The professor has very recently, while in Europe, procured many articles of especial interest as illustrating the
more advanced discoveries of the day. The more important
instruments owed by the college are as follows :

IN ELECTRICITY: Thompson's divided ring electrometer and reflecting
galvanometer; Wheatstone's bridge; British Association standard unit
of resistance; positive and negative electrophorus; Holtz machine, by
Ruhmkorff; Grove's galvanic battery of 40 elements; small induction
coil, giving spark of 2 inches, by Ruhmkorff; large coil with interrupter
giving spark of 17 inches; battery of 4 jars, *en cascade*, for the large coil;
Chester battery of 8 large elements; Bunsen galvanic battery of 60 elements; Foucault's electric lamp; collection of Geissler tubes; magneto-
electric machine; Morse register and relay magnet; Gaugain's tangent
compass; Lamont's electrometer for atmospheric electricity; pile of
Zamboni; large thermo-electric pile of 36 elements according to Marcus's
method of construction; jar with movable coatings; apparatus for pierc-
ing glass with electricity.

IN MAGNETISM: Lamont's magnetic theodolite for determining the
absolute intensity; additions to the theodolite for finding the absolute
declination; dipping needle for observations; magnetic engines.

IN LIGHT: Porte lumière; Duboscq's magic-lantern, adapted to the
use of either the electric or lime light; Marcey's sciopticon; complete
photographic apparatus; circle for demonstrating the laws of reflection,
refraction, polarization, &c.; Duboscq's apparatus for projecting upon a
screen all the phenomena of double refraction and polarization; solar
microscope with collection of objects; prism for the limiting angle; equi-
lateral flint-glass prism; hollow prism with compartments for different
liquids; polyprism; mounted achromatic lens; 3 bisulphide of carbon
lenses; total reflection fountain; spectroscopes.

IN HEAT: Ruhmkorfl's thermo-electric multiplier and pile; line pile
for showing calorific spectrum; collection of plates for diathermancy;
apparatus of Despretz for conduction; apparatus of Gay-Lussac for tension of vapors; apparatus of Senarmont for the conduction of heat in
crystals; thermometer with reservoir; weight thermometer; wet bulb
hygrometer; Breguet's metallic thermometer; differential thermometer;
apparatus of Tralles for maximum density of water; set of balls of different metals for specific heat; fire syringes of brass and of glass; Regnault's
hypsometer and hygrometer; Wollaston's eryophorus.

IN ACOUSTICS: From König of Paris: mouth-pieces, of several instruments; model of locomotive whistle; set of 10 diapasons with resonant cases; set of 19 Helmholtz resonators; double sirene of Helmholtz; 5 diapasons with resonators for the vowel sounds; large soufflerie for organ-pipes and sirene; 64 organ-pipes for demonstrating theory of vibrating air columns; sonometer with 8 cords; apparatus of Melde for vibrating cords; König's new apparatus for interference, shown by manometric flames; sets of plates for acoustic figures; ear and speaking trumpets; Dr. Auzoux's models of the ear and the larynx; wire-coil for showing the mode in which both light and sound waves are propagated, presented by Blake Brothers, of New Haven, Conn.; apparatus of Lissajou for showing vibrations by both the optical and graphical methods; Wheatstone's kaleidophone and wave apparatus; Schaffgotsch's apparatus; Quincke's apparatus for measuring wave length.

IN PNEUMATICS: Air-pumps with their apparatus; Magdeburg hemispheres and planes; apparatus for compressing air; apparatus for proving Mariotte's law.

IN STATICS AND DYNAMICS: Mechanical powers; Atwood's machine; whirling-table; pendulum, &c.

IN HYDROSTATICS AND HYDRAULICS: Hydrostatic bellows and press; hydrometers; Pascal's vases; Mariotte's flask; Prony's floater; apparatus for demonstrating the laws of spouting fluids; models of different forms of fountains; hydraulic ram; models of various forms of pumps; models of water-wheels.

FOR PRECISE MEASUREMENTS: Steel scales of English and French measures; graduated vessels of various measures and volumes; balances by Becker and other makers; spherometer by Buff and Berger; Wollaston's goniometer; theodolites, &c.

The following are some of the principal pieces recently received from London and Paris:

Mechanics.—Inclined plane of Galileo, Atwood's machine; apparatus of Bourdon Kater's pendulum; manometer of Bourdon; hydrostatic balance; gyroscope of Hardy and of Fessel; models of screws, of pendulums, and of escapements; large apparatus showing the principal transformations of movement-dividing machine.

Heat.—Volumometer of Say and of Regnault; pyrometer with dial; apparatus for the absolute dilatation of liquids; of Regnault, for dilatation of gases, both under constant pressure and under constant volume; of Dalton for tension of vapors; of Regnault for same; of Gay-Lussac

4 U

for tension of vapors below freezing-point; of Dalton for same in a vacuum; of Gay-Lussac for tension of mixed vapors and gases; of Dumas for density of vapors; of Gay-Lussac for same; of Regnault, with manometer, for density of gas; of Ritchie for emission and absorption of heat; of Jamin for the conduction of heat; calorimeter of Lavoisier and Laplace; of Regnault for specific heat by cooling; of same, large size; for specific heat by mixtures; of Favre and Silbermann for measuring heat of combustion; of Dupretz for measuring latent heat of vaporization; of Regnault, for measuring the elastic force of compressed air, and also of the tension of vapors both above and below 100 degrees C., complete; pyrheliometer of Pouillet; cathetometer, one meter in length, graduated; apparatus of Pouillet for measuring the compressibility of gases; of Simon for capillarity; of Bouligny, for the spheroidal state, complete; set of lenses, prisms, plates, &c., for the Melloni apparatus; large machine of Natterer for liquefaction of azote and of carbonic acid; Carré's air-pump, exhausting and condensing with sulphuric acid; reservoir.

Electricity and magnetism.—Large reflecting galvanometer of Weber with telescope; vertical differential galvanometer; apparatus of Ampère; electric planisphere; gas pile of Grove; secondary pile of Planté; large magnet of Jamin; Alliance magnets; electric machine; portable Grove's battery of fifty elements for the electric light; large electro-magnet for diamagnetism, rotation of polarized ray, &c.; Delezenne's circle; thermo-electric pile; set of resistance coils with bridge.

Acoustics.—Regnault's chronograph with clock; apparatus of Crovee for projection of wave motions.

Light.—Large heliostat of Silbermann; several forms of apparatus for projecting colored rings of thin plates; interference refractor of Jamin; circle, complete, of Jamin and Senarmont; combined polariscope and polarizing microscope; Biot's apparatus, complete, for rotary polarization, including Soleil's saccharometer; vertical lantern; prism of Dessains; large prism of Foucault; polariscope of Arago; photometer of Foucault; Becquerel's phosphoroscope; prisms of Senarmont, of Hartnack, of Jansen, of Rochon, and of Silbermann; apparatus of Delezenne; of Stokes; of conical prisms for caustics by reflection; of parabolic mirrors; of seven mirrors for recomposition of light; of two large piles of glass for polarization; a large Steinheil spectroscope with four prisms; large telemeter of Gautier.

Measurements.—Sets of French weights and measures of length and of capacity, dry and fluid.

ART DEPARTMENT.

The sum of $3,000 per annum, the gift of Miss Catharine L. Wolfe, of New York, has afforded the means for beginning a collection in this department, and it is proposed, as soon as practicable, to establish a professorship that shall control and develop the interests therein. The completion of Memorial Hall will afford a fine opportunity for the preservation and display of works of art.*

COLLEGE MAGAZINES AND PERIODICALS.

The Floriad was published by the Philomathean Society in the early years of this century. A few numbers of this, of 1811, are in the Boston City Library.

The Student's Album commenced in 1827. This contained essays and tales, literary and scientific items, and notices of new works.

The Parthenon and Academician's Magazine. The first volume of this dated in 1832–'33, and was continued two years.

Union College Magazine. Begun in 1860, under the joint auspices of the Philomathean, Adelphic, and Theological Societies, two editors being appointed by each. It is still continued, and has been from the first of very creditable literary character. Three numbers appear annually, one each term, and in the third year there was begun a series of portraits, one in each number, of distinguished men once connected with the college.

The Unionian was started about the same time as the latter, by members of the sophomore class. It subsequently assumed the quarto form and appeared monthly.

---

* A series of portraits of older members of the faculty is being made for the hall, and it is proposed to gather as large a collection as can be made of the portraits and busts of such as have been prominently connected with the history of the college.

The Spectator is under the care of a corps of editors from the advanced classes and representatives of the law and medical schools in Albany belonging to Union University. It is still published monthly, partaking more of the journalistic character, while the Union College Magazine represents the more literary features of the magazine.

THE SONGS OF UNION.

This feature of college literature deserves a passing notice. For many years they were floating waifs, and although some of them were productions of real merit, no collection was attempted until 18—, when they were published in a neat volume entitled " Carmina Concordiæ," under the editorial care of a member of the class of 1856.*

OTHER COLLEGE PUBLICATIONS.

No catalogues were published in the early years, and when the practice was begun it was limited to a broad sheet.

The regular annual issue began in 1820, and in 1832 a separate edition was published by the students. The latter usually contain the lists of secret and other societies not in the official edition. General catalogues were published in 1819, 1825, 1828, 1834, 1843, 1854, and 1868, the last two being in English, and the earlier ones in Latin.

---

* A few of these songs are perennial in their fragrance, and are always sung on festive occasions. This is especially true of the song to Old Union, composed by Fitzhugh Ludlow, of the class of 1856, and now deceased. It is always sung on commencement day, at the close of the graduating services. The hearty good will and feeling with which return-ing sons join in the grand chorus —

> "Then here's to thee, the brave and free,
> Old Union smiling o'er us,
> And for many a day, as thy walls grow gray,
> May they ring with thy children's chorus,"—

show that the gifted poet did not attune his lyre in vain.

The affairs of Union College have been frequently made a subject of report to the legislature, and these papers are scattered through the legislative records, and their titles are readily found in the general indexes. No complete series is known to exist in collected form.

Semi-centennial proceedings.

The semi-centennial proceedings in 1845 and 1854 were published, the former making 186 and the latter 122 pages. The semi-centennial proceedings of the Philomathean Society were published in 1849 in a volume of 154 pp.; quarter-centennial proceedings of *K. A.*, 1851.

The proceedings at the inauguration of presidents.

The exercises connected with the inauguration of Rev. Charles A. Aiken, D. D., June 28, 1870.

Proceedings at the inauguration of Rev. E. Nott Potter, D. D., as president of Union College, 1872.

Catalogues.

A catalogue of the college library has never been printed, but one of the Philomathean Society was printed in 1833, 1841, 1856, and 1863, and of the Adelphic Society in 1836, 1843, 1847, 1852, 1856.

These societies have repeatedly published catalogues of their members, the principal editions being, of the Philomathean, 1820, 1830, 1840, 1847, 1850; of the Adelphic, 1837, 1841, 1846, 1851; of the Delphian Institute, 1837, 1844.

General catalogues of the Phi Beta Kappa Society of Union College were published in 1827, 1833, 1852 1860.

Catalogues of secret societies have been published from
time to time, the principal of which were —

K. A. 1842, 1845, 1850, 1859, 1874.

Σ. Φ. 1838, 1846, 1850, 1853.

Δ. Φ. 1835, 1840, 1845.

Ψ. Υ. 1842, 1849, 1864.

X. Ψ. 1849, 1852, 1854.

0. A. Anti-Secret Confederation. 1847, 1850, 1853.

Fraternal Society. 1856.

θ. Δ. X. 1875.

Besides these, there have been published from time to
time and altogether, in amount equal to many volumes,
orations, addresses, and poems, delivered or read before the
college or its societies, by distinguished statesmen, scientists,
divines, and poets. The subjects embraced every field of
philosophy and literature, of political science and general
knowledge, and would, if collected, afford materials for a
publication of great permanent value.

The following are a portion of these publications:

Dr. E. Nott. Baccalaureate addresses. 1805, 1806, and
1811.

Samuel L. Mitchill. *Φ. B. K.* address. 1821.

Samuel Young. *Φ. B. K.* address. 1826.

Daniel D. Barnard. Senate of Union College. 1843.

Benjamin F. Joslin. *Φ. B. K.* 1833.

Thomas C. Reed. Discourse on Chester Averill. 1837.

D. D. Barnard. *Φ. B. K.* 1837.

William Kent. *Φ. B. K.* 1841.

Benjamin F. Butler. Senate of Union College. 1841.

Alfred B. Street. Poem. *Φ. B. K.* 1842.

John W. Brown. Poem. *Φ. B. K.* 1843.

William H. Seward. *Φ. B. K.* 1844.

Alonzo Potter. Semi-centennial address. 1845.

William B. Sprague. Theological Society. 1846.
John Todd. Literary Societies. 1846.
George P. Marsh. Literary Societies. 1847.
Ebenezer Halley. Theological Society. 1847.
Laurens P. Hickok. Theological Society. 1848.
Charles Sumner. Φ. B. K. 1849.
George W. Eaton. Literary Societies. 1849.
Tayler Lewis. Φ. B. K. 1850.
Thomas M. Clark. Φ. B. K. 1851.
Luther F. Beecher. Theological Society. 1851.
Benjamin N. Martin. Φ. B. K. 1852.
Ralph Hoyt. Poem. Φ. B. K. 1852.
Dr. E. Nott. Semi-centennial address. 1854.
Francis Wayland. Semi-centennial address. 1854.
George W. Clinton. Φ. B. K. 1857.
H. W. Warner. Semi-centennial. 1859.
D. H. Hamilton. Alumni address. 1861.
H. G. Warner. Φ. B. K. 1861.
William Tracy. Φ. B. K. 1862.
Robert J. Breckinridge. Φ. B. K. 1865.
Tayler Lewis. State rights. 1865.
Tayler Lewis. Heroic periods in a nation's history. 1866.
C. N. Potter. Φ. B. K. 1868.
Charles J. Jenkins. Φ. B. K. 1874.

GRANTS AND ENDOWMENTS.

(1) *Special public grants and endowments.*

By what authority granted.	Date of grant.	Land-grants.						Conditions and remarks.
		Extent.		Value.				
		Acres granted.	Acres now owned.	Value of lands sold.	Value of lands unsold.	Grants in money.	Value of other grants.	
Act of legislature, April 9, 1795.	1795	......	......	......	......	$3,750	..	For a library and apparatus.
Act of April 11, 1796.	1796	......	......	......	......	10,000	..	For buildings.
Act of March 30, 1797.	1797	......	......	......	......	1,500	..	Professor's salary.
Act of March 7, 1800.	1800	......	......	......	......	10,000	..	College edifice.
Act of March 7, 1800.	1800	5,500	..	$43,484	......	......	..	Support of president and professors.
Act of April 8, 1801, April 3, 1802	1801 1802	1,449	..	9,378		......		General purposes.

(2) *Special public grants of privileges producing funds.* [*]

Date of grant.	Name of grant—special object.	Amount.
By act of legislature, March 30, 1805.	Lottery for general purposes	$55,000
By act of April 13, 1814, and April 6, 1822.	Lottery for buildings.............	100,000
Do	Lottery to pay a debt	30,000
Do	Lottery for library and apparatus.	20,000
Do	Lottery for indigent students	50,000

[*] In former times, when banking privileges were monopolies difficult to secure and reasonably certain of large profits, the privilege of subscription to bank stocks was sometimes granted to educational institutions as a bonus to aid their funds. With this view, by an act passed April 2, 1813, the privilege of subscription to the stock of several banks was granted to Union College. The enterprise resulted in loss to the institution, instead of benefit.

(3) *Special grants from corporations.*

Grantors.	Date.	Amount.	Remarks.
Trustees of Schenectady.....................	1795	$24,954	General purposes.
Reformed Dutch Church of Schenectady...	1798	8,307	Do.
Old Academy	1798	564	Do.
Presbytery of Albany........................	1798	35	Do.

(4) *Individual benefactors.**

Names.	Date.	Amount.	Object, &c.
Original subscriptions.	1795	$7,433	General purposes.
Goldsbrow Banyer...........	1795	500	Do.
Abraham Yates, jr...........	1795	250	Do.
Eliphalet Nott...............	1853	760,523	For professorships, scholarships, library, astronomical observatory, &c., originally called $610,000, but now by accumulation inventoried at $760,523; all given by trust deed.
William and George Douglass and sister, Mrs. Cruger.	1860	5,000	For house for president and Mrs. Nott.
Divers small subscriptions ..	1859	2,970	For Memorial Hall.
C. N. Potter, Howard Potter	1874	35,000	Do.
H. G. Warner	1859	714	Prizes for good conduct, &c.
R. M. Blatchford............	1868	1,000	Prizes for oratory.
Do	1874	10,000	General purposes.
T. H. Powers...............	1873	3,000	Lectures.
Rev. Jas. C. Van Benschoten	1864	56	Books.
Rev. James A. H. Cornell...	1867	50	Library.
H. C. Van Vorst.............	1873	250	Do.
James Brown................	1873	10,000	Do.
Do	1873	100,000	General purposes
Catharine L. Wolfe..........	1873	5,000	For indigent students.
Do	1874	50,000	Do.
Do ....:.............	1875	3,000	For art purposes.
S. B. Brownell..............	1873	1,000	Professorship fund.
Do	1872	250	Physical apparatus.
William H. H. Moore.......	1874	1,928	Do.
Do	1874	1,000	Professorship fund.
Johnston Livingston	1875	1,000	Do.
C. S. Titsworth..............	1875	250	Do.
William Tracy..............	1873	1,000	Do.
R. D Hitchcock	1874	20	Do.
William H. Scheiffelin	1874	100	Do.
Hiram Gray	1875	100	Do.
Robert Earl	1875	200	Do.
Jno. A. Lansing	1875	50	Do
L. D. Baldwin	1875	100	Do.
William A. Righter..........	1875	250	Do.
James H. Cook.............	1875	50	Do.
G. D. G. Moore.............	1875	250	Do.
Alex. H. Rice	1872	400	Physical apparatus.
Henry C. Potter............	1872	400	Do.

(4) *Individual benefactors*—Continued.*

Names.	Date.	Amount.	Object, &c.
Henry R. Pierson	1872	$400	Physical apparatus.
Howard Potter	1872	400	Do.
William A. Whitbeck	1872	400	Do.
C. N. Potter	1872	400	Do.
Lemon Thomson	1872	200	Do.
Ansel E. Stevens	1872	25	Do.
Joseph W. Fuller	1873	10,000	Residence for president.
Uri Gilbert	1874	1,000	Gymnasium.
Hamilton Harris	1874	1,027	Do.
Divers small subscriptions	1874	2,873	Do.
Benjamin Brandreth	1845	250	Physical apparatus.
E. C. Delavan	1850	....	(The Wheatley collection of minerals and shells, valued at $20,000)
Benjamin Brandreth	......	....	(An air-pump, cost $150.)
Howard Potter	1870	....	(A painting, 6 x 8 feet, of Galileo before the Inquisition.)
Do	......	....	(Portrait of Dr. Wayland, late president of Brown University.)
Do	.	....	(A collection of shells, valued $200.)
Mrs. Harriet Gillespie	......	....	(A portrait of the late Professor William M. Gillespie.)

* Several of the large subscriptions since 1870 have been given in aid of the *Christian Union Endowment Fund*, as a measure tending to perpetuate and strengthen the unity which first suggested the name of the college, and which is expressed in the motto of the newly adopted seal: "In Essentials, Unity; in Nonessentials, Liberty; in all things, Charity." This fund is designed to be applied in the erection of new buildings, and in otherwise advancing the material interests of the college.

Unproductive funds, (not before mentioned.)

	Value.	Remarks.
Lands held for sale	$362,545	

THE GREATEST WANT OF THE COLLEGE.

Although Union College has ample facilities and considerable special endowments, it most needs funds that may be applied to general objects. The expenses of living have so increased that men receiving salaries deemed sufficient twenty years ago, cannot now afford to give their services without an increase of pay. A grant restricted to a particular use affords them no relief; and in this respect most of the older colleges of the country are in the same condition, and in one sense poor. A professional endowment-fund would, perhaps, confer the most substantial benefit to education of any measure that could be proposed, as by this means alone the highest talent can be secured in a faculty, and therein the greatest benefit conferred upon students.*

SUCCESSION IN THE SEVERAL PROFESSORSHIPS OF UNION COLLEGE.

Professors of Mathematics and Natural Philosophy.

1797, Col. John Taylor, A.M., died 1801.

1798, Cornelius Vander Heuvel, M.D., died 1799.

1800, Benjamin Allen, LL.D., resigned 1809.

1805, Rev. Thomas Macauley, D.D., resigned 1822.

1810, Frederic R. Hassler, resigned 1811.

1816, Rev. Francis Wayland, D.D., resigned 1826.

1822, Rev. Alonzo Potter, D.D., resigned 1826.

1827, Benjamin F. Joslin, LL.D., resigned 1837.

1831, Isaac W. Jackson, LL.D.

1839, John Foster, LL.D.

1865, John A. De Remer, adjunct professor of mathematics, resigned 1867.

1875, Isaiah B. Price, C.E., adjunct professor of physics.

Professors of Greek and Latin Languages.

1797, Rev. Andrew Yates, D.D., resigned 1801.

1801, Timothy Treadwell Smith, A.M., died 1803.

---

* At the commencement of 1874, it was proposed to raise a fund for endowing three professorships, of $30,000 each, to be named in gratitude to three old and faithful members of the faculty, the Jackson, Foster, and Lewis professorships, the first benefits to be allowed them as emeriti professores.

1807, Rev. Henry Davis, D.D., resigned 1810.
1818, Rev. Robert Proudfit, D.D., died 1860.
1849, Rev. Thomas C. Reed, D.D., resigned 1851.
1839, Rev. James Nichols, A.M., assistant professor, re-. signed 1841.
1846, Rev. Robert M. Brown, D.D., assistant professor, resigned 1846.
1852, Rev. John Newman, D.D., professor of Latin, resigned 1863.
1858, Benjamin Stanton, A.M., professor of Latin, died 1874.
1865, William C. Macy, A.M., adjunct professor of Greek, resigned 1866.
1863, Henry Whitehorne, A.M., professor of Greek.
1873, Rev. Robert T. S. Lowell, D.D., professor of Latin.

Professors of Moral and Mental Philosophy.

1814, Rev. Andrew Yates, D.D., resigned 1825.
1868, Nathan Hale, A.M., acting professor, resigned 1869.

Professors of Logic, Rhetoric, and Belles-Lettres.

1811, Rev. Thomas C. Brownell, D.D., resigned 1819.
1831, Rev. Alonzo Potter, D.D., resigned 1845.
1839, Rev. John Nott, D.D., resigned 1854.
1849, Wendell L'Amoreux, A.M., resigned 1853.
1863, Rev. Nathaniel G. Clark, D.D., resigned 1866.
1866, Rev. Ransom B. Welsh, D.D.

Professors of Chemistry and Natural History.

1814, Rev. Thomas C. Brownell, D.D., resigned 1819.
1822, Joel B. Nott, A.M., resigned 1831.
1834, Chester Averill, A.M., died 1836.

1837, Edward Savage, A.M., died 1840.
1839, Jonathan Pearson, A.M.
1855, Charles A. Joy, A.M., resigned 1857.
1858, Charles F. Chandler, LL.D., resigned 1865.
1865, Maurice Perkins, A.M.

Professors of Modern European Languages.

1806, Pierre Grégoire Reynaud, resigned 1822.
1826, Pierre Alexis Proal, D.D., resigned 1836.
1838, J. Louis Tellkampf, resigned 1843.
1849, Wendell L'Amoreux, A.M., resigned 1853.
1851, Elias Peissner, A.M., died 1863.
1865, William Wells, A.M.

Professors of Ancient Oriental Languages.

1827, Rev. John Austin Yates, D.D., died 1849.
1849, Tayler Lewis, LL.D.

Professors of Civil Engineering and Military Science.

1845, William M. Gillespie, LL.D., died 1868.
1868, Cady Staley, C.E.
1873, Capt. Thomas Ward, United States Army.

Professor of Anatomy and Physiology.

1849, Alexander M. Vedder, M.D., resigned 1863.

PRESENT FACULTY.

Rev. Eliphalet Nott Potter, D.D., President and Professor of Moral Philosophy, and of the Evidences of Christianity.

Tayler Lewis, LL.D., Nott Professor (No. 6) of the Oriental Languages, and Lecturer on Biblical and Classical Literature.

ISAAC W. JACKSON, LL.D., Nott Professor (No. 2) of Mathematics.

JOHN FOSTER, LL.D., Nott Professor (No. 8) of Natural Philosophy.

JONATHAN PEARSON, A.M., Professor of Agriculture and Botany.

HENRY WHITEHORNE, A.M., Nott Professor (No. 1) of the Greek Language and Literature.

WILLIAM WELLS, LL.D., Professor of Modern Languages and Literature.

MAURICE PERKINS, A.M., M.D., Nott Professor (No. 3) of Analytical Chemistry, and Curator of the Museum.

REV. RANSOM BETHUNE WELCH, D.D., LL.D., Nott Professor (No. 5) of Logic, Rhetoric, and Mental Philosophy.

CADY STALEY, A.M., C.E., Professor of Civil Engineering.

HARRISON EDWIN WEBSTER, A.M., Professor of Natural History.

REV. ROBERT T. S. LOWELL, D.D., Professor of the Latin Language and Literature.

CAPT. THOMAS WARD, U.S.A., Professor of Military Science and Director of Physical Culture.

ISAIAH B. PRICE, C.E., Adjunct Professor of Physics.

CHARLES JAMES COLCOCK, C.E., Tutor in Mathematics.

JONATHAN PEARSON, A.M., Treasurer and Librarian.

EDGAR MARSHALL JENKINS, ESQ., Assistant Treasurer and Registrar.

HENRY COPPÉE, LL.D., Lectures on History.

SYDNEY A. NORTON, A.M., M.D., Lectures on Experimental Physics.

REV. EDWARD A. WASHBURN, D.D., Lectures on Old English Literature.

REV. SAMUEL OSGOOD, D.D., LL.D., Lectures on German Literature and Modern Thought.

PROF. M. WENDELL L'AMOREUX, A.M., Lectures on the South European Languages and Literature.

PROF. SELAH HOWELL, A.M., Lectures on English Literature.

Preparatory Department.

CHARLES STORRS HALSEY, A.M., Nott Professor, (No. 7,) Principal of the Classical Institute.

SAMUEL BURNETT HOWE, A.M., Adjunct Nott Professor, (No. 4,) Principal of Union School and Superintendent of the Schools of Schenectady.

Statistics of attendance and graduation.

Years.	Freshmen.	Sophomores.	Juniors.	Seniors.	Total.	Left without graduating.	Graduated, (A. B.)	Years.	Freshmen.	Sophomores.	Juniors.	Seniors.	Total.	Left without graduating.	Graduated, (A. B.)
1796								1836	36	75	100	77	288	16	71
1797						1	3	1837	30	72	99	105	306	34	91
1798						1	6	1838	17	65	109	102	293	26	93
1799						6	14	1839	22	48	94	122	286	32	106
1800						9	7	1840	31	72	80	112	295	19	105
1801						8	7	1841	36	62	96	84	278	16	80
1802						10	8	1842	28	64	77	96	265	24	90
1803						4	17	1843	32	54	81	75	242	19	72
1804						6	15	1844	27	45	69	81	222	21	81
1805						11	13	1845	32	59	73	79	243	15	72
1806						6	14	1846	24	66	88	111	289	16	90
1807						9	11	1847	32	72	96	99	299	17	80
1808						12	18	1848	30	78	118	102	328	19	79
1809						17	29	1849	27	59	96	140	322	25	109
1810						23	27	1850	9	64	89	104	266	23	77
1811						45	28	1851	8	50	97	102	257	20	78
1812						24	29	1852	8	38	83	106	235	33	69
1813						15	45	1853	16	50	68	89	223	26	62
1814						19	40	1854	28	62	70	81	241	31	50
1815						11	39	1855	41	89	87	83	300	33	51
1816						12	50	1856	62	97	122	102	383	39	66
1817						6	43	1857	35	98	132	130	395	56	78
1818						17	52	1858	41	104	121	145	411	59	91
1819	13	59	89	79	240	22	56	1859	42	105	134	159	440	60	77
1820	16	58	85	96	255	26	65	1860	40	92	133	148	437	58	98
1821	17	46	84	88	235	21	66	1861	36	80	109	140	390	75	75
1822	19	53	72	90	234	16	76	1862	46	72	89	124	352	63	66
1823	10	44	81	74	209	13	62	1863	16	66	76	99	285	48	62
1824	7	39	76	86	208	11	79	1864	25	73	81	98	294	48	57
1825						20	62	1865	21	52	72	84	249	40	46
1826						9	70	1866	27	43	59	71	223	41	36
1827						16	68	1867	28	43	46	60	199	30	38
1828						10	69	1868	17	37	40	43	162	29	25
1829						14	82	1869	17	37	46	56	164	29	18
1830						9	96	1870	22	25	26	29	114	18	26
1831						13	76	1871	27	23	18	24	103	20	24
1832						5	70	1872	20	25	20	14	89	19	13
1833				87		18	69	1873	33	23	44	33	134	12	18
1834	33	46	83	66	228	17	64	1874	39	32	28	28	160	24	21
1835	26	78	75	89	268	17	88	1875							14

Students in civil engineering.

Years.	Students.	Graduates, (C. E.)	Years.	Students.	Graduates, (C. E.)	Years.	Students.	Graduates, (C. E.)	Years.	Students.	Graduates, (C. E.)
1857	18	3	1862....	21	6	1867....	19	12	1872....	9	4
1858	18	9	1863....	18	2	1868....	23	9	1873....	23	5
1859	28	4	1864....	20	7	1869....	22	8	1874....	33	13
1860	26	6	1865....	22	4	1870....	20	6	1875....	....	14
1861	26	9	1866....	23	9	1871....	14	6	.		

Students in analytical chemistry.

Years.	Number of students.	Years.	Number of students.	Years.	Number of students.	Years.	Number of students.
1857	7	1862........	26	1867........	35	1872........	12
1858	9	1863........	29	1868........	16	1873........	18
1859	26	1864........	21	1869........	21	1874........	18
1860	20	1865........	14	1870........	27	1875........	......
1861	30	1866........	16	1871........	14		

5 U

Home-residences by States of alumni of Union College.

Dates	Alabama	Arkansas	California	Connecticut	Delaware	Dist. of Columbia	Florida	Georgia	Illinois	Indiana	Iowa	Kansas	Kentucky	Louisiana	Maine	Maryland	Massachusetts	Michigan	Minnesota	Mississippi	Missouri	Nebraska	New Hampshire	New Jersey	New York	North Carolina	Ohio	Pennsylvania	Rhode Island	South Carolina	Tennessee	Texas	Vermont	Virginia	Wisconsin	Foreign States	Total
1797																									4												4
1798																								1	7												7
1799																									19												20
1800																									16												16
1801																	1								15			1	2					1			15
1802																									15				1				1			1	18
1803																	1							1	17				1								21
1804																									17				2				1				21
1805																									22				1				1			1	24
1806																									17				1								20
1807																	1								18				1								30
1808																	1								27				1	2							46
1809				2													3							1	43				1								52
1810				1													1								58				1								73
1811				1													1								68	1			1								61
1812				2													1								45				1				3				59
1813				2									2				3								58				1				5				50
1814				6													2								45					2							62
1815				4		2											2							1	42								2			2	49
1816				5				1									7						5		47	1		1						4			69
1817				4	1			1						1			4	1					1		41			2		3			6	2			78
1818				4				1					1	1	1		8							3	51		1	3		2	1		2	4		2	91
1819				3		1							1	1			6						1	3	55			7					4	2			87
1820				7		1											7							2	60			3			1						92
1821				6	1			4									7						1	8	47	3	1	1					3	4		1	75
1822																									63												
1823																									39												

1824				3				5									7	1		1			1	2	63	2		2		1			2				90
1825				2	1			6								2	5							2	54	2	1	3		2			1	1			82
1826				2													8						1	3	59	1		2					2			1	79
1827	1			9	1										4	2	9						2	2	44	1		2		3			3	1			84
1828	1			6		1		4							1	1	5	1					2	1	48	1	1	1		1			2	1		1	79
1829	1			9				4								1	5	1		1			3	1	57	1	1	2		2			2	4		1	96
1830					1	1								1		5	6	1					3		61	2		9		4			7	4			105
1831	1			2				2								3	4						1	5	60			5		2			2	2			89
1832				4				3						1	2	1	8						2	3	47			1					2			1	75
1833				2				2							1		9						3	1	63	1	1	2					2				87
1834				5									1		1	1	6						9	2	55								1				81
1835				5					1						2	5	8						1	2	76			1					2	1		1	105
1836				1											1	2	11							1	61			4			1		5				87
1837				3													9							3	100	1	1	3					4	1			125
1838				5										1			5	1					2		97	2		3					2	1			119
1839				3						1							6						3		119	2		3					1				138
1840				7				1					2		1		3						1	2	98		2	2					3	2			124
1841				3													7						1		74			4					6	1			96
1842	1			1	1								1				1	1					1	3	100			1					3				114
1843																	4	2					1		77		2	3					2				91
1844	3			2				1							1		7						1	1	83				1				1			1	102
1845	1			1												2	2	1					1		75			2								2	87
1846				3											1		5						2	1	85		5						1	1		2	106
1847								1	1								4								79	1	2	4					3			2	97
1848				2				2					1				1						1		85		1	4					1				98
1849	1			1				1							1		1							3	116	1	3	4					1			1	134
1850				2	1										1	1	2			1				2	76	1	3	8	1				1				100
1851				3	1												5	5		3	1			2	68		3	5			1		1				98
1852				1	1				2						1		4	2					1	4	68	3		8			1		1	2		3	102
1853				4		1		1	2					1			6						1		51		1	13	1				1	1	1	3	88
1854				1	1				1	1	1					1	3	1		1			1	3	54			4			2		4	1	1		81
1855					1								1		2		5				2			2	58	2		8						3			84
1856				1	2				1		1				7	1	7						1		71	1	3	3					4		1	1	105
1857				2					1		1			1	3	3	7						1	5	93		5	6	1	1			3		1	3	137
1858	1		1	2	3				3	2	1		1	1	6		4			1			2	2	103		3	10		1			6		2	2	157
1859	1			2	2			1	3				1		2	1	6				3			3	94	1	1	13				1	4		2	1	141
1860				4	1			1		5	3		1		4	1	10	1						1	102		6	10	2		3	1			3	3	162
1861		1		2	2	1		1		1			1	5	3	1	2	2	1		1		1	3	110		3	12			1		2		1	2	159
1862					2		1		2			1	3		2	1	5	4					1	1	90	1	5	11					4			1	135
1863				3	1	1			7		1		5		1	2	3	1					2	5	69		1	7					2		1		112
1864			2	1				1	2		1						5				1			4	76		7	6					2	1	1	2	112

Home-residences by States of alumni of Union College—Continued.

Dates	Alabama	Arkansas	California	Connecticut	Delaware	Dist. of Columbia	Florida	Georgia	Illinois	Indiana	Iowa	Kansas	Kentucky	Louisiana	Maine	Maryland	Massachusetts	Michigan	Minnesota	Mississippi	Missouri	Nebraska	New Hampshire	New Jersey	New York	North Carolina	Ohio	Pennsylvania	Rhode Island	South Carolina	Tennessee	Texas	Vermont	Virginia	Wisconsin	Foreign States	Total
1865		1		1					5	1	1		1		2		1				1		1	2	58		6	6					4				88
1866				1	1				3	2	1						4	2			1			1	63		3	1					2	1			80
1867					1				2	2		1		1	2		1	3						1	54		3	5	1				2	1			80
1868				3		1			2				2		1	1	1								50		1	5		1	1	1	1			1	65
1869				2						2	1				1					1				1	40			2			1				1		55
1870									2	2							1				1			1	35		2	1					3				50
1871											1			1	2							1		3	37		2	4	1								50
1872				1					1	1						1					1		1		27		1	1									36
1873		1												1	1										28			2					2				35
1874				2													1								37		1	2		1			1				45
1875				2													1	1							34										1		43
	12	3	3	175	26	10	1	46	146	19	12	2	24	17	58	45	284	31	1	10	11	1	62	110	4,539	31	81	240	21	28	11	3	138	45	16	42	6,189

HONORARY DEGREES CONFERRED BY UNION COLLEGE.

From the year 1795 to the year 1875, a period of eighty years from the incorporation of the college, the total number of honorary degrees conferred was as follows: A.B., 70; A.M., 241; D.D., 219; LL.D., 97; being an average of less than 1 A.B., 3 A.M., between 2 and 3 D.D., and between 1 and 2 LL.D., per annum. The attention of the board having been called by the president of the college to the fact that the tendency of late years had been to greatly increase the number of honorary degrees conferred, the conferring of honorary degrees was omitted on the occasion of his inauguration. At the meeting of the board of trustees incident to the following commencement it was ordered that only by unanimous consent could an honorary degree be conferred upon any person whose name had not been submitted ninety days previously, and the Hon. Judge Nott, of the Court of Claims, gave notice of a resolution to be offered at the next meeting of the board, limiting, also, the number of degrees to be conferred. It was thought just that these restrictions should not be imposed until after certain names presented to the board, with the anticipation from former precedents of a favorable result, had been acted upon. The resolution offered by Judge Nott, seconded by the president of the college, and unanimously adopted by the board, is as follows:

Resolved, That the committee on degrees hereafter, until otherwise instructed, will report to the board only two persons for the honorary degree of Doctor of Literature and Laws, and three persons for the degree of Doctor of Divinity.

The first commencement after the adoption of the above

resolution, was that of June, 1875; the terms of the resolution were then and will henceforward be strictly complied with.

PREPARATORY DEPARTMENT.

•An academic school in connection with Union College was established by President Nott immediately after his election in 1804. The teachers in this school were appointed by him, and the principal was recognized by the laws of the college as a member of the faculty. This academic school became popular and extensively useful for many years—the pupils prosecuting the irstudies therein greatly exceeding in number the students prosecuting their studies in the classes in college. Among the distinguished men who successively held the office of principal in this school, which was conducted in the two lower rooms of the west college, were Rev. Dr. Thomas Macauley, Rev. John Mabin, Rev. Daniel H. Barnes, Hon. Aaron Clark, and Rev. Dr. Ichabod S. Spencer.

On the 7th of April, 1818, an act was passed authorizing the revival and re-organization of the Schenectady Academy; under this act the academy was re-organized by the election of a board of trustees on the 1st day of April following.

Three departments were instituted by the board: the first embracing the course of studies requisite for admission into college; the second calculated for the education of those youths who do not wish to go through a college course; the third adapted to the instruction of young ladies. The first department instituted by the board succeeded to and was intended to embrace the object for which the academical school aforesaid was founded, and that school was merged in said department.

The Rev. Dr. Nathan N. Whiting was appointed principal of the academy, the late Lewis Beck instructor in the English department, and Gen. Jacob Gould instructor in the female department. Mr. William Beattie succeeded as principal of said school to Rev. Mr. Whiting, and on his resignation in 1828, Daniel Fuller was appointed principal.

To the Schenectady Academy, the Schenectady Lyceum, incorporated under the general law for the incorporation of academies, succeeded, and continued until the re-organization of the schools in 1854.

By an act passed April 9, 1854, the "board of education of the city of Schenectady" was constituted, with ample powers to re-organize the schools of the city, and also to purchase of the trustees of Union College "the building heretofore known as West College for the use of said common schools and an academical department."

In accordance with this law the trustees of Union College sold the West College to the city in 1854. At the same time an arrangement was made by which so long as the city reserved two suitable rooms for the academical or classical department, the college, under provisions of Dr. Nott's trust-deed, would pay the salary of the principal of said department and give free tuition to such pupils as entered Union College from said classical department.

The first principal of the classical department was Prof. Benjamin Stanton, who died in 1874. The second was Prof. Henry Whitehorne, now professor of Greek in Union College; and the third and present incumbent is Prof. Charles S. Halsey.

In 1872 a large and commodious building was purchased by Union College for the use of the classical department, which was re-organized under the name of the Union Classical Institute. The premises are valued at $15,000.

Its affairs are managed by ten persons, called the "board of education." They are elected by the legal voters of the city, and serve for a term of two years. Three prizes have

been established, of the value of $50 each, for the best essays
in writing and speaking. Instruction is given by one male
and four female teachers; and the course of instruction is
divided into three terms in a year of thirteen weeks each.
Present attendance, 60 males and 75 females.

UNION UNIVERSITY.

Union College, we have seen, was located at Schenectady
because the intelligent statesmen and scholars of the period
saw the immediate necessity of a large collegiate institution
for the center of the State, and one which should, as far as
possible, utilize all interests, harmonizing and combining them
into a union tending to produce strength and permanence.
It was quite natural that the capital should, under the circumstances, be claimed as a suitable location on account of
its ease of access at that time by water, and the fact that it
was the political center of the State. General Schuyler, of
Albany, was prominent among those who were convinced of
the advantage of placing an institution for the academic
training of young men far enough from the capital to be free
from its diverting attractions, and yet not so distant as to be
difficult of access to this great central power of the State. To
him Schenectady, with its favorable location on the Mohawk
and its comparative retirement, so conducive to successful
study, seemed just the spot, and his influence thrown into the
balance decided the question in its favor.

About forty years after the incorporation of Union College
the people of Albany conceived the idea of establishing a
series of post-graduate institutions at the capital, and began
by the founding of a medical school. For the following suc-
cinct history of the medical college, the law school, and the
Dudley Observatory, we are largely indebted to an outline

prepared by one long connected with these Albany institutions.*

ALBANY MEDICAL COLLEGE.

At a meeting of citizens of Albany held April 14, 1838, the following resolution was adopted: ·

Resolved, That this meeting deem it expedient to establish a medical college in this city, and to endeavor hereafter to obtain an act of incorporation from the legislature.

, To give immediate effect to this resolution, Samuel Stevens and George Dexter, esquires, were appointed a committee to prepare articles of association; a building for the use of the proposed institution was obtained from the city authorities, and the sum of ten thousand dollars was subscribed as preliminary to its more ample endowment. A few weeks after, Judge Harris, on the part of the board of trustees, reported the appointment of the following persons as the members of the first faculty of the Albany Medical College, viz: Drs. Alden March, James H. Armsby, Ebenezer Emmons, Henry Green, and David McLachlan. The Hon. Amos Dean was at the same time appointed professor of medical jurisprudence. Soon after Dr. David M. Russ was added to the faculty, and George Dexter, esq., was made treasurer of the board of trustees.

---

* These historical summaries of the Albany institutions forming a part of Union University, as now recognized by law, are inserted in this connection to complete the account of the university, and as the best that can be had at this moment. They were prepared by Dr. James H. Armsby, recently deceased, and from his own intimate connection with their origin and management, he could not speak of them with that freedom which another person acquainted with the facts might justly have done. They are not, therefore, presented in this connection as a model of full histories, and when completed for the final report they will embrace more precise dates and statistics than are at hand as these pages go to press.

F. B. H.

Among distinguished members of the medical profession who have filled the vacancies that have from time to time been caused by the death or resignation of members of the original faculty, are Drs. Thomas Hun, Gunning S. Bedford, James McNaughton, Lewis C. Beck, T. Romeyn Beck, Howard Townsend.

The holding of surgical cliniques was introduced at an early period in the history of the college, and has been continued to the present time.

The museum of the college, originally consisting of the private anatomical and pathological collections of Drs. March, Armsby, and McNaughton, presented by them to the college, has been constantly increasing in extent and value, and is now not inferior to that of any medical college in the country. Dr. March made a liberal bequest to the college for the care and preservation of his collection.

The college still occupies the old Lancaster school building, the use of which was granted by the common council of the city of Albany, but extensive additions have been made to the original edifice.

In the immediate vicinity of the college is the kindred institution, the Albany Hospital. This noble charity, which receives the liberal support of the citizens of Albany, furnishes gratuitous treatment to all indigent persons who apply for it. Many of the professors are connected with it, and the students are admitted without charge to its cliniques, lectures, and practice.

ALBANY LAW SCHOOL.

The law school was incorporated under an act of the legislature in the spring of 1851. The trustees met on the 21st of April, and organized the school by the following appointments: President of the board of trustees, Thomas W. Olcott, esq.; secretary, Orlando Meads, LL.D.; professors,

Ira Harris, LL.D., Amasa J. Parker, LL.D., and Amos Dean. LL.D.; president of the faculty, Hon. Greene C. Bronson.

At its origin the law school was dependent upon the almost unaided efforts of its professors. It had no endowment, and it was with difficulty that lecture rooms for its use could be procured. The first lectures were given in the third story of the Albany Exchange, formerly occupied by the Young Men's Association. The first class numbered only twenty-three students. While the school was thus suffering from the need of a permanent location, the trustees of the medical college generously offered a piece of land lying south of the building which they occupied, as a site for a lecture hall, and by the effort of friends a sum was raised sufficient to defray the expense of its erection. When in 1860 more extensive accommodations were required, the necessary additions and provisions were made at the expense of the professors. Since then the number of students has rapidly increased.

At the present time more ample accommodations are again needed, and the faculty look with confidence to the liberal citizens of Albany for assistance in erecting a new and larger edifice.

THE DUDLEY OBSERVATORY.

This institution was incorporated by the legislature in March, 1852. It was named in honor of Charles E. Dudley, as an acknowledgment of the munificent contributions made to its endowment by his widow, Mrs. Blandina Dudley. Prof. O. M. Mitchel selected the site and Gen. Stephen Van Rensselaer gave the land on which the observatory building was erected. The trustees have since purchased additional land, amounting in all to eight acres, about half a mile north of the capitol. The building was completed in 1854, from plans furnished by Prof. Mitchel.

The observatory was inaugurated on the 28th of August, 1856, at the meeting of the American Association for the Advancement of Science. The inaugural address on that occasion was delivered by Edward Everett. A eulogy on Charles E. Dudley was also pronounced by Washington Hunt.

Mrs. Dudley's donations, including bequest, amount to more than one hundred and five thousand dollars. The aggregate donations amount to more than two hundred thousand dollars. More than one hundred thousand dollars have been expended on the buildings, instruments, grounds, and other objects, and seventy thousand dollars invested as a permanent fund for the support of the institution.

The observatory is amply furnished with instruments procured, without regard to expense, from the best European and American artists; of these the Olcott meridian circle is worthy of especial note.

Since its connection with Union University, three buildings have been erected for the several departments of a physical observatory.

The meteorological department of the latter is already in operation, under the direction of Gen. Albert J. Myer, chief of the United States Signal-Service.

In 1869 a charter was granted for an astronomical observatory at Schenectady, under separate trustees, but in the interest of the college. The act contemplated a loan from the State, but this failing, the project was given up, and the more recent connection of the Dudley Observatory at Albany, under a university charter, has supplied, in the ample equipment of a first-class observatory, every needed facility in this department.

INDEX.

	Page.
Academy, gift of	57
Academy, Schenectady	6, 8
Addresses, titles of published	54
Aiken, Rev. Charles A	22
Albany Law-School	74
Albany Medical College	73
Alumni association	42
Alumni, home residence of	65
Analytical chemistry, students in	65
Anatomy and physiology, professors of	61
Ancient Oriental languages, professors of	61
Apparatus	48, 57, 58
Armsby, Dr. James II	73
Art department	51
Attendance and graduation, statistics of	64
Bibliography of faculty	19
Blatchford oratorical medals	46, 57
Botanical garden	25
Brown, James, fund given by	47, 57
Brownell, Rev. Thos. C	16, 19
Buildings, former	11, 12, 15
Buildings, present	23
Carmina concordiæ	52
Catalogues	53
Charlotte County, memorial from	5
Chemistry, analytical, students in	65
Chemical laboratory	39
Chemistry and natural history, professors of	60
Christian Union endowment fund	58
City hall	12
City schools, classical department	71
Civil engineering	38

	Page.
Civil engineering, department of	38
Civil engineering, course of study in	39
Civil engineering, professors of	61
Civil engineering, students in	65
Classical studies, comparison of periods	26-31
Clinton College, project of.	5
Coe memorial fund	47
Collections in natural history	47
College magazines and periodicals	51
Colonnades	23
Commencement exercises, place of holding.	9
Course of study	25
Course of study, comparison of periods	26-37
Decline of college during the war	22
Degrees, honorary	69
Delavan, E. C., gift of	47, 58
Douglass, W. and G., gift of	57
Dudley, Mrs. Blandina, bequest of	76
Dudley Observatory	75
Edwards, Rev. Jonathan	9, 19
Endowments, early	11
Faculty, present	61
Foster, Prof. John	18
Foster, Prof. John, collections of apparatus by	47
Fuller, Joseph W., gift of	58
Gardens	25
Gillespie, William M	18, 21, 38
Graduation, statistics of	64
Grants and endowments	56
Greek and Latin, professors of	59
Grounds, description of	24
Gymnasium	24
Hassler, Prof. F. R	18
Herbarium from Dr. George T. Stevens	47
Hickok, Rev. Laurens P	16, 19
Home residence of alumni	65
Honorary degrees	69
Hooker, Philip, architect	12
Inauguration proceedings	53

Page.

Individual benefactors 57
Ingham prize 46, 57
Jackson, Prof. Isaac W... 17, 20
Jackson garden 25
Joslin, Dr. B. F.. 17, 20
King's College... 5
Laboratory, chemical 39
Lancasterian School... 12
Land-grants 56
Legislative grants 56
Lewis, Prof. Tayler.. 18, 21
Libraries.. 46
Literary societies 41
Logic, rhetoric, and belles-lettres, professors of................... 60
Lottery grants...12, 13, 14, 56
Lowell, Rev. R. T. S.. 21
Macauley, Rev. Thomas 16
McClelland, Dr. John, benefactions of................................. 44
Magazines and periodicals... 51
Mathematics, professors of 59
Maxcy, Rev. Jonathan.. 9
Memorial hall 23
Meteorological station 76
Military instruction.. 41
Military science, professors of 61
Modern European languages, professors of............................. 61
Moral and mental philosophy, professors of........................... 60
Name of college, origin of... 8
Natural history, collections in...................................... 47
Natural philosophy, professors of.................................... 59
Newman, Rev. John... 18
North College 23
Nott, Rev. Eliphalet 10, 19
Nott, Joel B.. 17
Nott, Rev. John 17
Nott scholarships 45, 57
Olcott meridian circle.. 76
Olivier models.. 38
Organization and early history....................................... 5

Page.

Pearson, Jonathan... 17, 20
Peissner, Prof. Elias........................... .... 18, 21
Periodicals, college.. 51
Perkins, Prof. Maurice 18
Philosophical department....................................... 47
Portraits, collection of 51, 58
Potter, Rev. Alonzo.... .... 16, 20
Potter, C. N. and H., gift of....................... 57
Potter, Rev. Eliphalet Nott.................................. 22
Prefatory note 3
Preparatory department.. 70
Preparatory department, professors in 63
Present buildings 23
Present faculty... 61
Present grounds 24
President's house... 24
Prize essays 46
Prize speaking 46
Prizes and medals 46
Proal, Rev. P. A.. 17
Professors of over ten years' service 16
Professorships, succession in 59
Proudfit, Rev. Robert 16
Publications by faculty...................................... 19
Ramée, M., plans by.. 13
Recent history... 22
Reed, Rev. Thomas C... 17
Reformed Dutch Church, gift of 57
Residence of alumni 65
Reynaud, Grégoire.. 16
Romeyn, Rev. Dirck 7
Schenectady Academy 70, 71
Schenectady, early project of a college at.................. 5
Schenectady, gift of trustees of............................. 57
Schenectady Lyceum 71
Scholarships... 43, 57
Scientific studies, comparison of periods................... 32-37
Secret societies... 42
Semi-centennial of college................................... 17

	Page.
Semi-centennial of Dr. Nott's presidency	19
Semi-centennial publications	53
Signal-service station	76
Site of permanent college	13
Smith, Rev. John Blair	9, 19
Societies, college	41
Songs of Union	52
South college	23
Special prizes	46
Stevens, Dr. George T., herbarium of	47
Students from other colleges	15
Study, comparison of periods	26-37
Succession in professorships	59
Tryon County, memorial from	5
Union Classical Institute	71
Union University	72
Vedder, Dr. A. M	18
Wants of the college	59
Warner prize	46, 57
Wayland, Rev. Francis	16, 20
Webster, H. E., contributions of	47
Wells, Prof. William	18
West college	12
Wheatley collection	47, 58
Wolfe, Miss Catharine L., benefactions of	43, 51, 57
Wolfe, John David	43
Yates, Rev. Andrew	16
Yates, Rev. John A	17

6 U